THE

BASEBALL BUFF'S

BATHROOM BOOK

VOLUME ONE

CARL H. JOHNSON

The Baseball Buffs Bathroom Book
Copyright 2016 Carl H. Johnson
ISBN 978-1519696403

Cover by

Distributed by Carl H. Johnson and Associates.

Dedication/Acknowledgments

To my wonderful wife and editor, Janice Longfellow, who provided me with insight, expert opinion and guidance through this project and the preceding ones and without whom I would not have the patience and/or perseverance to have completed any of them. To our Grandchildren and Beta Readers, Alex and Sierra Maggs, otherwise known as The Review Crew, who faithfully read and provide editorial comment and criticism of everything I write.

To Beatrice Silverstein, my High School Latin and English Teacher, who was one of the most dedicated and effective teachers I have ever known and who encouraged me to write sports those many years ago.

To my old friend Kate Flora, author of the Thea Kozak and Joe Gunther mysteries, who I have known since the days when 'many were written but none were published', for her inspiration.

And, finally, to Abner Doubleday, Alexander Cartwright or whoever actually invented this game that makes the Baseball Season the best season of the year for most of the citizens of this great country and more of the world every year, and who never knew how popular their simple game would become.

CONTENTS

SECTION 1

The New York Yankees' John Wetteland is the only pitcher in history to save all four games of a single World Series. He did it against the Atlanta Braves in 1996 and was named Most Valuable Player of that Series. Six other pitchers, Roy Face, Kent Tekulve, Jonathan Papelbon, Mariano Rivera, Troy Percival and Sergio Romo, have saved three games in a single Series.

THE GAS HOUSE GANG AND THE 1934 WORLD SERIES

The 1934 St. Louis Cardinals were a different team. Made up of an unusual mix of hard playing, probably overly aggressive players, many of whom, including the Dean Brothers, Dizzy and Paul 'Daffy', came from the south or southwest, they muscled their way to a 95-58 season in 1934 to win the National League pennant and meet the Detroit Tigers in the World Series.

There are differing stories about how the team got the nickname the Gas House Gang. Baseballreference.com says that ' The nickname was given them as a way of describing the enjoyment with which they seemed to play the game, along with the aggressive attitude they took that always seemed to give them dirty uniforms, making them resemble the grease stained clothing worn by car mechanics.'

Gas houses were facilities that produced gas from coal usually located in the worst part of cities. History.com has a less flattering explanation for the nickname, saying it was due to ' The team's close resemblance to the rowdy, dirt streaked assemblage of thugs who hung around the Gashouse District on Manhattan's East Side.'

Whatever the reason for the name, the team had a successful year in 1934 with Jay 'Dizzy' Dean winning the MVP Award and 30 games, the last pitcher to reach that number in the National League. The Tigers were led by Mickey Cochrane, who won the

American League MVP Award, with a .320 average, the third highest average on his own team and just two homers and 76 RBI's. Teammate Charley Gehringer, at .356 and 11 homers and 127 RBI's led the team in hitting and Hank Greenberg at .339 with 26 homers and 139 RBI's was second. The Tigers were favored to win the Series.

When the teams took the field for the first game of the World Series, there were eight players in the starting lineups, four on each team, that would eventually make it to the Hall of Fame. The Cardinals had Player/Manager second baseman Frankie Frisch, left fielder Ducky Medwick, pitcher Dizzy Dean and Leo Durocher, who would make the Hall as a Manager. The Tigers had catcher Mickey Cochrane, second baseman Charlie Gehringer, first baseman Hank Greenberg and left fielder Goose Goslin, the 2,3,4 and 5 hitters in their lineup.

In Game 1, at Detroit, Dizzy Dean started for the Cards against General Crowder for the Tigers. The Cards got two in the second on a single by center fielder Ernie Orsatti and an error by second baseman Gehringer on a ball hit by Dean, an error by third baseman Marv Owen on a ball hit by Pepper Martin and a two run scoring single by right fielder Jack Rothrock. They got another in the third, aided by two more errors by the Tigers, to make it 3-0.

Detroit got one back in their half of the third when Gehringer singled in Jo Jo White, who had walked, to make it 3-1. Medwick got a solo homer in the fifth to make it 4-1.

The Cards went up 8-1 in the sixth when Firpo Marberry relieved Crowder for the Tigers and Dean led off with a double and was driven in on Martin's single. After Rothrock bunted Martin to second, Medwick singled to drive him in. First Baseman Ripper Collins then singled to right and Chief Hogsett replaced Marberry on the mound for the Tigers. Catcher Bill DeLancey singled to drive in the Cards last run and make it 8-1.

The Tigers would get one in the sixth and add another on a homer by Greenberg in the eighth but the final was 8-3 St. Louis. Dizzy Dean went the route for St. Louis, giving up just three runs on eight hits for the win.

Game 2 was a pitchers' duel between Detroit's Schoolboy Rowe, 24-8 during the regular season, and the Cards Bill Hallahan. The Cards led 2-1 going to the last of the ninth when Fox singled, was sacrificed to second by Rowe and scored on a single by pinch hitter Gee Walker to tie the game. Bill Walker, no relation to Gee, came on in relief of Hallahan and got out of the inning.

The game went to the last of the twelfth still tied and, after getting the first batter, Walker walked Gehringer and Grenberg and Goslin then singled to drive in Gehringer and the Tigers had won the game 3-2 and the Series was tied at one game each going to St. Louis.

At home, the Cards got one in the first of Game 3, when Martin led off with a triple and scored on a sac fly by Rothrock. They added another in the second when Collins singled, went to third on DeLancey's double and scored on a sac fly by starting pitcher Paul Dean, to make it 2-0. They got two more in the fifth on a double by Martin, a triple by Rothrock and a single by Frisch and it was 4-0. The Tigers got on the board with a single by White and a triple by Greenberg in the ninth but that was the scoring and the Cards won 4-1 to go up 2-1 in the Series. Dean went all the way for the win giving up just the one run on eight hits.

Detroit won Game 4, 10-4 behind Eldon Auker, who threw a complete game though giving up four runs on 10 hits. The Tigers got three in the third and five in the eighth in winning easily, with a barrage of 13 hits off five different Cardinal pitchers. Greenberg had four hits for Detroit, including two doubles and three RBI's while Rogell drove in four with two singles. Greenberg also stole home in the eighth inning while Owen was stealing second.

Tommy Bridges, who had lost Game 3, two days earlier, started on the mound for the Tigers and went the whole route in Game 5, giving up just one run on seven hits. Dizzy Dean went eight for the Cards, giving up three runs, two earned, on six hits as the Tigers won 3-1 to go up three games to two.

The Tigers got one in the second when Fox doubled to center to score Greenberg and added two in the second on a lead off homer by Gehringer and a sacrifice fly by Green scoring Rogell who had gotten to third on an error by center fielder Chuck Fullis. DeLancey homered in the seventh for the Cardinals for their only run and the teams went back to Detroit with the Cardinals facing elimination, down 3-2.

Paul Dean, who had won Game 3, faced Schoolboy Rowe, who had won Game 2, in Game 6, back in Detroit. The Cards got one in the first when Rothrock doubled and scored on Medwick's single. The Tigers came back in the third, as White walked, tried to steal second and ended up on third when the throw got away. Cochrane singled to drive him in and tie the game at 1-1. In the fifth, Durocher singled and was sacrificed to second by Dean, then scored on Martin's single. When the throw to home to try to get Durocher went wild, Martin ended up on third and scored on Rothrock's ground out to short and the Cards led, 3-1.

The Tigers tied it at 3-3 in the sixth as White walked and Cochrane singled to put men on first and third. Gehringer then reached on an error by Dean and White scored. Greenberg then singled to drive in Cochrane with the tying run.

In the top of the seventh, Durocher doubled to deep center and Paul Dean singled to drive him in with what turned out to be the winning run in his second victory of the Series as the Cards forced a seventh game with a 4-3 victory.

Game 7 was anticlimactic as the Cardinals humiliated the Tigers at home, 11-0 on 17 hits, scoring seven runs in the third inning on four singles, three doubles and three walks. They added two in the sixth, with the big hit a triple by Medwick.

When Medwick slid into third, he injured third baseman Marv Owen with his hard slide and the Detroit fans began to throw things on the field. Commissioner Kenesaw Mountain Landis ordered Medwick removed from the field to quiet the crowd so the game could go on.

The Cards got two more in the seventh with Durocher getting a triple and Rothrock a double. The Tigers used six pitchers including Rowe, who relieved starter Auker in the third after pitching a complete game the day before and faced just three batters, giving up a double and a single.

Dizzy Dean got his second win of the Series, pitching a complete game shutout while giving up just six hits. The Dean brothers had won all four games for the Cardinals, Dizzy winning Games 1 and 7 and Paul winning Games 3 and 6.

The Gas House Gang had surprised everyone and gone all the way. The Tigers came back to win the 1935 World Series, beating the Chicago Cubs in six games.

SECTION 2

There have been 292 No Hitters and 23 Perfect Games in Major League history. Nolan Ryan has the most no hitters with seven and eleven of the others have been pitched by a combination of two or more pitchers. The one you will read about here is different than all the rest.

A ONE OF A KIND GAME

Former Major League pitcher Ken Johnson was born on June 16, 1933, in West Palm Beach, Florida. He passed away, on November 21, 2015, at age 82. Johnson pitched 13 years in the Major Leagues, from his debut with the Kansas City Athletics in 1958 until1970 when he ended his career with the Montreal Expos, his seventh team.

As a right handed starting pitcher, he had a mediocre career, winning 91 and losing 106 and compiling a career 3.46 ERA. Not exactly the stuff legends are made of but he did accomplish one thing that no other pitcher in baseball history has ever done. He pitched a nine inning no-hitter and lost the game, 1-0.

On April 23, 1964, he started on the mound for the Houston Astros against one of his old teams, the Cincinnati Reds, in Colts Stadium. In the first inning, after striking out Pete Rose for the first out of the game, he walked Vada Pinson but got out of the inning with no scoring.

In the bottom of the first, former Chicago White Sox second baseman and future Hall of Famer, Nellie Fox, finishing his career with the Astros, doubled for Houston but was then thrown out trying to steal third base.

In the second and third innings both Johnson and the Reds' Joe Nuxhall got the sides in order. In the bottom of the fourth, Astros first baseman Pete Runnels singled to center but center fielder

Johnny Weekly hit into a double play to end that threat.

In the top of the fifth, Johnson walked the Reds left fielder Bob Skinner for his second walk of the game but got out of the inning with no scoring.

The Astros threatened in the last of the seventh when Fox singled, Runnels reached on an error but Weekly hit into another double play to end that rally. In the eighth the Astros wasted a lead off double by center fielder Jim Wynn and left him stranded on second.

The game went to the ninth, 0-0, with Johnson still throwing a no hitter. He got Nuxhall, who, surprisingly, hit for himself, to ground to third. Rose then hit a ground ball back to Johnson who threw wild to first allowing Rose to reach second with one out. Third baseman Chico Ruiz then grounded out with Rose going to third. Center fielder, Vada Pinson, then hit a grounder to second which Fox misplayed and Rose scored the game's first and what turned out to be the only run.

Johnson then got another future Hall of Famer, right fielder and cleanup hitter, Frank Robinson, for the last out of the top half and the game went to the last of the ninth with the Reds up 1-0 but Johnson's no-hitter still intact.

In the last of the ninth, Nuxhall, who had given up just five hits, got shortstop Eddie Kasko on strikes and got Fox to ground to short for the second out. Runnels then reached on an error by first baseman Deron Johnson but Nuxhall struck out Weekly for the third out and the Reds had won a game without a hit and Ken Johnson had become the only pitcher in baseball history to lose the game while throwing a complete game no-hitter.

Only 5,426 fans were on hand for the game which lasted just one hour and 56 minutes. Johnson walked just two batters and had nine strikeouts en route to his no-hit loss. The two teams, between them, had just one less error than hits in the entire game as they both committed two miscues, Houston's two in the ninth costing Johnson the game.

The Astros finished in ninth place that year, with a record of 66-96 and the Reds finished in third at 92-70. Johnson's opponent Joe Nuxhall, who pitched a complete game, five hit shutout, finished the season at 9-8.

Johnson won 11 and lost 16 in 35 starts that year with a 3.63 ERA. He was traded from the Houston Astros to the Milwaukee Braves on May 23 of the 1965 season and had his best year in the Majors going 16-10 between the two teams with a 3.21 ERA in 37 starts.

Ken Johnson may not have been one of the greatest pitcher to play the game but his performance that day and the lack of support from his teammates combined to make it a one of a kind game, a distinction I am sure he would rather not have had.

Ichiro Suzuki holds the record for the most hits in a single season in baseball history, with 262 in 2004. In addition to this single season record, he also had the 10th, 18th, 56th and 66th highest total in a single season.

JOE DIMAGGIO

The Yankee Clipper, Joe DiMaggio, was, in my opinion, the best all around ball player I ever saw play the game. I was born in 1938 and saw Willie Mays, Ted Williams, Stan Musial, Sandy Koufax, Nolan Ryan and many of the other greats from the 1940's on. I even saw Connie Mack manage the Philadelphia Phillies in one of his last games against the Yankees in Yankee Stadium.

Joe was with the Yankees from his debut in 1936 until 1951 but spent three of those years, 1943-1945, in the Army in World War II. Like many players of this era, he spent most of his time in the military instructing physical education and playing baseball but did his duty to his country.

He was born in Martinez, California, on November 25, 1914 and played three years for the San Francisco Seals of the Pacific Coast League from 1933 to 1935, hitting .340, .341 and .398. If the averages weren't high enough, he had a 61 game hitting streak in 1933, his first year in organized ball. This streak is the second longest streak in Minor League history, second only to Joe Wilhoit's streak of 69 in 1919. The Yankees bought DiMaggio from San Francisco for $25,000. and five players and he made his debut with them on May 3, 1936.

In his first four years with the Yankees, 1936-1939, the team won the American League Championship and went on to win the World Series, the first of nine times he would be on a World Championship team. He was also in the World Series in 1942 but the Yankees lost that year to the St. Louis Cardinals. He was named to the American League All Star team every one of the thirteen years he played.

He had a career batting average of .325 and slugging percentage of .579 and won the American League Batting Championship in 1939 and 1940, hitting .381 and .352. He was the American League's Most Valuable Player in 1939, 1941 and 1947 and led the league in home runs in 1937 and 1948 with 46 and 39. He was elected to the Baseball Hall of Fame in 1955.

In addition to his hitting ability, Joe was a fine defensive center fielder. Teammate Yogi Berra, one of the greatest catchers of all time, once said of DiMaggio, ' He never did anything wrong on the field. I'd never seen him dive for a ball, everything was a chest high catch and he never walked off the field. ' He was an extremely graceful and gifted athlete who could run at top speed while looking like it was effortless which made him a great base runner. The fact that he hit 10 or more triples in seven different seasons is testament to his base running ability and speed.

Much has been written about his 56 game hitting streak in 1941. Prior to this accomplishment, the longest a player had ever gone with at least one hit in every game was the 44 game streak of Wee Willie Keeler in1897. This record is one of very few baseball records which will probably never be broken. Pete Rose hit in 44 consecutive games in 1978 and is the only player since George Sisler in 1922 to break 40 games.

More amazing than the streak was his record at the plate for the entire season. While hitting .357 and winning the Most Valuable Player Award, he came to the plate 617 times, including 76 bases on balls, and struck out just 13 times in that entire season, a mind boggling one strike out in every 47.5 at bats.

His brothers, Dominic and Vince were also major league center fielders. Dom, three years younger than Joe, was with the Red Sox his entire career, from 1940-1953, and spent the years 1943-1945 in the service like Joe. He was a lifetime .298 hitter and an

All Star seven times. At 5'9" and 168 pounds and wearing eye glasses he was dubbed the Little Professor.

Vince, two years older than Joe, played center field for the Red Sox, Cincinnati Reds and Pittsburgh Pirates and had a .249 life time batting average. He was named to the National League All Star Team twice, in 1943 and 1944, when his more famous older and younger brothers were in the military. The DiMaggio brothers were the only three players in baseball history with the surname DiMaggio.

Joe DiMaggio was a charismatic figure and one of, if not the most, popular of all the Yankees. He was a great representative of the game both on and off the field. Whenever anyone talks about the greatest all around players of all time, DiMaggio's name is always near the top.

As New York Mayor Ed Koch once said of him ' He represented the best in America. It was his character, his generosity, his sensitivity. He was someone who set a standard every father would want his children to follow.'

If you saw the commercial Gatorade made for Derek Jeter's retirement in 2014, you saw Jeter touch the sign at the entrance to the field from the clubhouse in Yankee Stadium that says ' I'd like to thank the Good Lord for Making Me a Yankee '. That was Joe DiMaggio's quote and summarizes his life, career and dedication to the game and the team.

SECTION 4

Twenty-eight hitters in Major League baseball history have averaged over .400 for a single season. The last was Ted Williams of the Boston Red Sox who hit .406 in 1941. The highest average for a single season was .440 posted by Hugh Duffy of the old Boston Beaneaters in 1894.

THE OTHER DIMAGGIO'S STREAK

Every baseball fan knows about the longest hitting streak in Major League Baseball history, Joe DiMaggio's remarkable feat of hitting safely in 56 consecutive games from May 15 to July 16, 1941. During the streak, Joe hit .409, with 91 hits in 223 at bats. Coincidentally, that same year, Red Sox slugger Ted Williams hit .406 for the entire season, one of three times he hit .400 or better.

Joe DiMaggio's record still stands today and may be the only baseball record besides Cy Young's career 511 wins to remain unbroken forever.

On August 9, 1949, another hitting streak was broken and fell short of the Yankee Clipper's 56 games. The Boston Red Sox center fielder, Dominic Paul DiMaggio, Joe's younger brother, went into a game against the Yankees at Fenway Park with a 34 game hitting streak on the line.

Dominic had begun his streak on June 26 against the St. Louis Browns when he went 3-5 with three singles. He had hit .352 and scored 35 runs in the 34 games going into that August 9 game against the Yankees.

The Yankees Ace right hander, Vic Raschi, was on the mound for New York that day. Raschi had a 15-6 record coming into the game and was facing the Red Sox Ellis Kinder, who was 12-5. Both Raschi and Kinder pitched complete games with the Red Sox winning 6-3 to make their record 61-44.

The Sox were in third place five games behind the first place Yankees. Joe McCarthy was the Red Sox Manager and Casey Stengel led the Yankees. The Yankees would go on to win the pennant and beat the Dodgers four games to one in the World Series. The World Series win was the first of five consecutive World Series wins for the Yankees.

The Sox would finish in second place, one game behind the Yankees, after losing to the Yankees on the last day of the season 5-3. The same two pitchers, Raschi and Kinder were on the mound in that final game with Raschi finishing the season at 21-10 and Kinder at 23-6.

With his streak on the line, Dom led off the first inning for the Sox and grounded out to Phil Rizzuto, the Yankees future Hall of Fame shortstop. He also led off the third inning and flied out to his brother, future Hall of Fame center fielder, Joe Dimaggio. In his third at bat, he led off the fifth inning and was struck out by Raschi. In the seventh, he hit a ground ball back to Raschi, who threw him out at first.

In the eighth inning he came to the plate with his last chance at extending the streak and perhaps going on to match or better his brother's all time record. Tom Clavin, author of the book, 'The DiMaggio Brothers', described that at bat in the New York Times of May 11, 2013 as follows; ' Down to his last at bat, he sent a screaming line drive to the outfield that Joe caught, preventing Dominic from coming any closer to Joe's record 56 game streak. ' The streak was over, ended by a shoestring catch made by his brother, the record holder.

In addition to the Yankee's Rizzuto, DiMaggio and Raschi, Yankee great Hank Bauer, who played on seven Yankees World Championship teams and later managed the Orioles to a World Championship, played right field that day and had two home runs.

The Red Sox lineup had Johnny Pesky playing third and batting second, followed by Ted Williams, who hit his 28th homer in the third, with Vern Stephens at short batting fourth. Second baseman Bobby Doerr batted fifth and first baseman Billy Goodman, right fielder Al Zarilla, Catcher Birdie Tebbetts, who homered in the second, and pitcher Kinder rounded out the lineup. Both Kinder and Raschi had base hits for their teams that day.

Ted Williams went 2-4 and raised his batting average to .348. He would end the season in second place in the batting race behind Detroit Tiger third baseman George Kell. Both Kell and Williams hit .343 but Kell's .3429 beat out Williams' .3428 for the title in the closest race in baseball history.

Dominic, the youngest of three DiMaggio brothers to play center field in the big leagues, played for the Sox from 1940 until 1953. In addition to his brother Joe, the oldest of the three brothers, Vincent Paul DiMaggio, played ten years in the big leagues with the Boston Braves, Cincinnati Reds, Pittsburgh Pirates, Philadelphia Phillies and New York Giants. He had a career average of .249.

Dominic enlisted in the Navy in World War II and missed the 1943-1945 seasons. When he returned in 1946, he hit .316 and batted in 73 runs as a lead off hitter.

The year after the streak, 1950, Dom hit .328 with 193 hits and, in 1951, hit .296 with 189 hits. During that 1951 season, he had another streak, hitting safely in 27 games. In 1952, he played in 128 games and hit .294. After being benched by Red Sox Manager Lou Boudreau, in 1953, he retired from the game.

He had a career .296 batting average and was named to seven all star teams. At 5'9", 168 pounds, and wearing glasses, he was dubbed the Little Professor and that nickname followed him through his career. He was a fine defensive player as well as being an extremely productive lead off hitter but played in his brother Joe's shadow for most of his career. He was named to the Red Sox Hall of Fame in 1995.

SECTION 5

Cy Young won 511 games in his career, the most by any pitcher in the history of baseball, and Walter Johnson won 417, the second highest total. The five pitchers with the most wins all time were all right handers. Warren Spahn won more games than any other left hander in the history of the game, 363.

SPAHN, SAIN AND PRAY FOR RAIN

In 1948, the Boston Braves won the National League Pennant but lost the World Series to the Cleveland Indians in six games. On September 14 of that year, Sports Editor Gerald Hern, of the Boston Post, published a poem that went like this;

'First we'll use Spahn, then we'll use Sain,
Then an off day, followed by rain.
Back will come Spahn, followed by Sain,
Followed, we hope, by two days of rain.'

This poem was inspired by the performance of Warren Spahn and Johnny Sain, the workhorses of the National League's Boston Braves pitching staff who were in the process of carrying the Braves on their shoulders into the World Series.

In an unbelievable stretch of twelve days beginning with a Labor Day doubleheader, the duo had won eight games without losing. On Labor Day, Spahn won the first game of the twin bill, pitching 14 innings and Sain came back and won the second game. There followed two days off for rain and Spahn won the next day and Sain pitched the win the following day. Three days later, Spahn won again and Sain won the next day. Then, after a day off, Spahn won the first game of a doubleheader and Sain won the second.

I don't know if this is the greatest achievement by a pitching twosome in the history of the game but I would doubt if any pair ever put together such a stretch. Going into Labor Day, the

Braves had a 2 ½ game lead over the Dodgers and Cardinals but ended the season with a 91-62 record, 6 ½ games ahead of the second place Cardinals.

In the World Series, Sain bested Bob Feller in the first game throwing a complete game 2 hit shutout to win 1-0. Spahn took the loss in Game 2 lasting only 4 innings as Cleveland tied the series at 1-1. Cleveland won game 3 by a 2-0 score and Sain came back in game 4 and went all the way but lost 2-1. The Braves stayed alive in game 5 winning 11-5, with Spahn throwing the last four innings in relief. A crowd of 86,288, the largest in World Series history to date, watched this game.

Cleveland went on to win the series, taking game 6, 4-3 with Spahn again coming on in relief in the eighth.

For the series, Spahn and Sain were each 1-1 with Sain pitching 17 innings and giving up just 2 runs and Spahn 12 innings and 4 runs. In the six game series, the Braves used a total of just 6 different pitchers and either Spahn or Sain appeared in 5 of the 6.

Warren Spahn was born on April 23, 1921, in Buffalo, New York and Johnny Sain on September 25, 1917, in Havana, Arkansas. Both made their Major League debuts with the Boston Braves in April of 1942, five days apart, and both enlisted in the military after the 1942 season, Spahn in the Army where he participated in the Battle of the Bulge and was awarded a Purple Heart and Sain in the Navy Air Corps. Both returned to the Braves for the 1946 season.

In that 1948 season, the pair won 39 games while losing 27 and Spahn pitched 16 complete games and 257 innings and Sain an amazing 28 complete games and 315 innings. Between 1946 and 1950, the two won 181 games and lost only 129 with Sain winning over 20 games 4 times and Spahn 3 times.

In their careers, both pitchers completed more than half of all the games they started with Spahn completing 382 of his 665 starts and Sain completing 140 of his 245 starts.

Sain was traded to the Yankees in 1951 and the duo was broken up. When the Braves moved to Milwaukee in 1953, Spahn went with them. He pitched a total of 20 years for the Braves and had 13 seasons with 20 or more wins. His total of 363 wins is the most by a left handed pitcher in the history of the game. In 1963, at the age of 42, he compiled a 23-7 record with the Braves. He made the All Star Team 14 times, won the Cy Young Award in 1957 at the age of 36 and was elected to the Hall of Fame in 1973.

In the 1957 World Series, which the Braves won 4 games to 3, Spahn pitched the first game and lost to Whitey Ford 3-1 then came back and pitched a complete game 10 innings against the Yankees in game 4 and won the game 7-5. The next year, the Braves played the Yankees in the series again and this year the Yankees won, 4-3. Spahn beat Ford 4-3 in game 1, throwing a 10 inning complete game then returned with a complete game shutout 3-0 in game 4. He started the sixth game but, after being tied 2-2 at the end of 9, lost it in the tenth 4-3.

After leaving the Braves, Sain spent 4 years, mostly in relief, with the Yankees, playing on World Series Championship teams in 1951, 1952 and 1953. He spent his final big league year with the Athletics before retiring in 1955. He went on to become one of the most successful pitching coaches in the history of the game and was the Pitching Coach on World Championship teams with the Yankees in 1961 and 1962 and with the Detroit Tigers in 1968.

Warren Spahn and Johnny Sain had remarkable careers beyond 1948, but they and that magical pennant run will always be remembered with ' Spahn, Sain and Pray For Rain' which was more popular then in Boston than Sweet Caroline is today.

SECTION 6

In the first World Series, played in 1903, the Boston Americans beat the Pittsburgh Pirates 5 games to 3. The Americans used just 3 pitchers in the eight games with Bill Dineen pitching 35 innings, Cy Young 34 and Tom Hughes 2.

SEPTEMBER 28, 2011

Fans all across the country were treated to one of the most exciting nights in the history of baseball on September 28, 2011.

In the American League, the Red Sox, who four weeks ago looked like a cinch to be in the Playoffs, nine games ahead of Tampa Bay for the Wild Card, were looking at possible elimination after losing 19 of 26 games in the month. Tampa Bay, on the other hand, who had all but been forgotten four weeks ago, had an opportunity to sneak into the playoffs thanks to the Red Sox fold. While everyone was focusing on the fact that the Red Sox had lost their 9 game lead by winning only 7 of 19 games, the more amazing statistic was that the Rays had made up a nine game deficit while winning just 16 of 26 games.

While this drama was unfolding, the Atlanta Braves and St. Louis Cardinals entered the final day tied for the National League Wild Card with identical 89-72 records. On August 31, the Braves had been in first place in the Wild Card race, 8 ½ games ahead of the Cardinals. The Braves had started September with a record of 80 wins and just 55 losses, while the Cardinals, with a record of 72-64 seemed to be out of the race.

Over their last 27 games, the Braves managed to win only nine while losing 18, slightly better than the Red Sox 7-19 for September so far but bad enough so that the Cardinals made up the 8 1/2 game deficit, by winning 18 of their last 26, and went into the final game in a tie with the Braves for the Wild Card.

The Braves were playing the Phillies, needing to win to stay alive after the Cards, playing earlier, behind a complete game two hit shutout by Chris Carpenter, had beaten Houston 8-0 to go one half game up.

The Red Sox vs Orioles game, the Yankees vs Rays game and the Braves vs Phillies games were all on television at almost the same time. What more could a baseball fan want for the last day of the season?

The Phillies trailed the Braves 3-2, in Atlanta, going into the ninth inning and Chase Utley hit a sacrifice fly to tie the game and send it to extra innings. The game stayed tied until the 13th inning when a bloop single by Hunter Pence drove in the winning run for the Phillies for a 4-3 win, sending the St. Louis Cardinals to the World Series and sending the Braves home for the season. This exciting finish was taking place while the Red Sox and Rays were fighting for their seasons and it was all on national television.

Down in Baltimore, the Red Sox scored one run in each of the third, fourth and fifth innings while the Orioles got two in the third. Lester pitched the first six, giving up two runs on four hits and left ahead 3-2. After a one hour and twenty-six minute rain delay, Aceves and Bard got through the seventh and eight both without allowing Baltimore to score.

In the top of the eighth, the Sox blew an opportunity to add an insurance run when, with Boston ahead 3-2, Scutaro singled to right off Pedro Strop. Crawford then hit a double into the left center field gap. Scutaro was unsure whether the ball had been caught or it had dropped in and hesitated getting to third even though being waved around by the coach. He was thrown out at the plate on a perfect relay from Adam Jones to J. J. Hardy to Matt Wieters. It appeared that Scutaro would have scored fairly easily had he not hesitated.

As a result, the Sox went to the last of the ninth ahead 3-2, instead of 4-2, with their closer, Papelbon who had 31 saves and had only blown three save attempts, coming in.

While this was going on, the Yankees built a 7-0 lead over Tampa Bay after five innings and the Red Sox situation was looking good. The Rays then came up with six runs in the eighth inning, three of them coming on a homer by third baseman Evan Longoria. In the last of the ninth, trailing 7-6, the Rays Dan Johnson hit a pinch hit homer to send the game into extra innings. They remained tied through the top of the 12th inning and went to the last of the 12th within minutes of the Sox going to the last of the ninth.

In Baltimore, Papelbon got the first two Orioles in the ninth, Adam Smith and Mark Reynolds, on swinging third strikes and things were looking even better for the Sox. Then Chris Davis hit Papelbon's first pitch for a double and Buck Showalter put Kyle Hudson in to run for him. The next batter, Nolan Reimold, went to two and two and Papelbon was one pitch away from sending the Sox to the playoffs. On the next pitch, Reimold hit a ground rule double to score Hudson and knot the game at 3-3 and put the winning run on second. Robert Andino then hit a soft liner into short left that Carl Crawford could not quite reach, Reimold scored from second and the game was over, the Sox had lost the game, 4-3 .

A few minutes later, down in Tampa Bay, in the last of the twelfth, Evan Longoria, facing the Yankees 11th pitcher of the game, Scott Proctor, with the game tied 7-7, hit a home run down the left field line to perhaps the shortest reachable part of the stands in fair play in the ballpark for a walk off home run to send the Rays to the Playoffs and end the Red Sox season.

Baseball had just witnessed the most incredible end to a baseball season that anyone was ever likely to see. To make it all the more incredible, fans across the country had been able to watch all three games on television as they came to an end within minutes of each other.

Red Sox fans were in shock. Just four weeks ago their team was in first place and Sox fans were looking ahead to another

American League East win. It was inconceivable that they would not be in the playoffs. Sox fans, after the wins in 2004 and 2007, had been getting ready for another World Series.

Of course, the Wild Card Cardinals then came from behind, time after time, to win the World Series, beating the Texas Rangers, in seven games, but that's another story for another time.

On June 23, 1917, Babe Ruth, pitching for the Red Sox against the Washington Senators, walked Eddie Foster to lead off the game and was ejected from the game when he argued the call. Ernie Shore relieved Babe and, after Foster was thrown out stealing, got the next 26 outs without a hit for the first combined no-hitter in baseball history.

SATCHEL PAIGE

Satchel Paige was born Leroy Robert Paige on July 7, 1906 in Mobile, Alabama. Prior to the integration of baseball, he pitched in the Negro League and various Independent Leagues from 1927 until 1947 and was signed to a contract by Bill Veeck's Cleveland Indians on July 7, 1948, his 42nd birthday.

Two days later he made his Major League debut as the oldest rookie in the history of baseball and went two innings in relief against the St. Louis Browns, holding them scoreless while giving up two hits and striking out one.

On August 3, he pitched before what was at the time the largest crowd ever to see a Major League Game. 72,562 fans crowded Cleveland Stadium that day as he beat the Washington Senators, 5-3, pitching seven innings, giving up three runs on seven hits, for the win. The victory put the Indians in a tie for first place with the New York Yankees.

On August 13, he pitched a complete game, 5-0, shutout against the Chicago White Sox at Comiskey Park in Chicago, to put the Indians in first place by ½ game over the now second place Philadelphia Athletics. On August 20, before a new record crowd of 78,382, he pitched another complete game shut out of the White Sox, winning 1-0, to put the Indians three games up on the Boston Red Sox.

The Indians went on to win the pennant and beat the Boston

Braves in the World Series four games to two. Satchel only pitched in one of the games of the series in relief but finished the regular season with a 6-1 record after pitching in 21 games, starting seven times and compiling a 2.48 ERA.

In his 20 years of pitching before he came to the Major Leagues, Satchel had pitched for such Negro League teams as the Birmingham Black Barons, Chicago Giants, Cleveland Cubs, Pittsburgh Crawfords, Kansas City Monarchs, New York Black Yankees and the Homestead Grays. He pitched year round most years, pitching in winter ball and even pitched in the Cuban Winter League in 1928.

The two years before he was signed by Cleveland, he barnstormed with Bob Feller, traveling around the country in two planes leased by Feller. It was the Bob Feller All Stars against the Satchel Paige All Stars wherever they went. Feller's team had Major Leaguers such as infielders Mickey Vernon, Phil Rizzuto and Ken Keltner, outfielders Jeff Heath, Charlie Keller and Sam Chapman and catcher Jim Hegan. The pitchers included Feller, Bob Lemon, Dutch Leonard, Johnny Sain and Spud Chandler.
Satchel did not do as well his second year with the Indians, winning four and losing seven with a 3.04 ERA. He pitched in 31 games, starting only five, for a total of 83 innings.

After the 1949 season, he was released by the Indians on February 17, 1950 and played in the Negro League for $800. per game. In 1951, when his former boss Bill Veeck bought the St. Louis Browns, he signed Satchel on July 14, at age 45, and he pitched in 23 games with three wins and four losses.

The next year, he appeared in 46 games, at age 46, and won 12 and lost 10, with a 3.07 ERA. He was used primarily in relief that year but started six games. In those six starts, he threw three three complete games and two of them were shut outs. He was named to the American League All Star team that year. Despite a poor start in 1953, he appeared in 57 games, ending up with three wins and nine losses. He was named to the All Star team again at age 47.

He was released by the Browns, who had moved to become the Baltimore Orioles that year, on February 2, 1954. From 1956 until 1958, from age 50-52, he pitched for the Miami Marlins in the AAA International League and, in 1961, for the Portland Beavers in the AAA Pacific Coast League, at age 55.

In 1965, Charlie Finley, owner of the then Kansas City Athletics, signed him to pitch one game and, on September 25, at age 59, he started against the Boston Red Sox, pitching three scoreless innings, giving up just one hit, a double to Carl Yasztremski, before being removed. Finley, ever the showman, had invited several veteran Negro League players to be introduced before the game. Satchel became the oldest player ever to pitch in a Major League game.

In addition to having a number of effective regular pitches, Satchel developed the 'hesitation pitch' where he stopped his motion just before releasing the ball to throw off the hitter's timing and the 'eephus' pitch which was a high arcing change-up.

The nickname Satchel apparently came from when he was a porter carrying satchels at the local train station as a youngster.

Satchel's family has a web site devoted to the pitcher. Among other things, many quotes attributed to Satchel are listed on that page. Included among them are ' My pitching philosophy is simple, you've got to keep the ball off the fat part of the bat' and, my favorite, and I think most appropriate, is ' I ain't never had a job, I just always played baseball.'

Satchel Paige always did play baseball and he enjoyed every minute of it. He did not set records in his brief career although if he had begun at a younger age he might have. He was inducted into the baseball Hall of Fame in 1971 by the Negro League Committee recognizing his unique contributions to the game.

SECTION 8

Babe Ruth's record of 60 homers in one season, in 1927, was broken by Roger Maris with 61, in 1961. Since then, three different players have hit more than 60, including Barry Bonds with 73, in 2001, and Mark McGwire with 70, in 1988. McGwire also had 65 in 1999 and Sammy Sosa had 63, in 1999, 64, in 2001 and 66 in 1998. Maris still holds the American League record.

ROGERS 'RAJAH' HORNSBY

Rogers Hornsby's information in the National Baseball Hall of Fame calls him ' the greatest right-handed hitter in baseball history '. In the six year period from 1920 through 1925, The Rajah, of the St. Louis Cardinals, won the batting title in the National League every year. In that period, his lowest average was .370 in 1920 and his highest was .424 in 1924.

He hit over .400, three times in that period, including .401 in 1922 and .403 in 1925, to become the only player other than Ty Cobb ever to hit over .400 three times in different seasons. His cumulative batting average for those years was a mind boggling .402.

In addition to his unbelievable average, he won the Triple Crown twice in that period, in 1922, when, in addition to leading the league in hitting, he had 42 homers and 152 runs batted in and, in 1925, when he again led the league in hitting and had 39 homers and 143 RBI's. He led the league in slugging percentage 1925 when he had a .756 percentage, bettered in baseball history only by Babe Ruth, Barry Bonds and Lou Gehrig. He also won his seventh National League batting title in 1928 with a .387 average. He was voted Most Valuable Player in the National League in 1925 and 1929.

In addition to his batting titles, he led the National League in slugging percentage nine times, in on base percentage nine times, in total bases seven times, in runs scored five times and in runs batted in four times. He was a hitting machine who once said of himself ' Every time I stepped to the plate with a bat in my hands, I couldn't help but feel sorry for the pitcher '. In those six years from 1920 to 1925, everyone must have felt sorry for the pitchers.

Hornsby was born in Winters, Texas on April 27, 1896 and made his debut with the Cardinals on September 10, 1915, at the age of 19. When he debuted, he was 5'11" and weighed just 135 pounds. After his first year, he worked at putting on weight and, after that, played at 175 pounds, giving him more power at the plate.

He played 13 years for the Cardinals, (including a 46 game stint in 1933 when he came back to St Louis briefly and hit .325), playing every position except pitcher and catcher, but mostly at second, short and third, and compiled a .359 average with 2,110 hits. In 1925, when he won the Triple Crown, and 1926, when he hit just .317, he was Player Manager of the team for part of both years. In 1926, as Player Manager, he led the Cardinals to the National League pennant and beat the New York Yankees in the World Series.

He was traded to the New York Giants on December 20, 1926, for Frankie Frisch and Jimmie Ring. The great Frisch once said of Hornsby 'He's the only guy I know who could hit .350 in the dark.'

He was with the Giants just one year, 1927, serving as Player Manager for part of the year and hitting .361 before being traded to the Boston Braves for Shanty Hogan and Jimmy Welsh. With the Braves, in 1928, while also serving as Player Manager for part of that year, he still managed to hit .387.

On November 27, 1928, he was traded to the Chicago Cubs for five players and $200,000. In his first year with the Cubs and last full year as a player only, he hit .380 with 39 homers and 129 RBI's and led the Cubs to the pennant and the World Series where they were defeated by the Philadelphia Athletics.

He took over as Player Manager of the Cubs from mid season in 1930 through 1932 and, at age 34, began to limit his play. In August of 1932, he was released by the Cubs and spent part of 1933 as Player Manager of the Cardinals, playing 46 games and hitting .325. Midway through the season, on July 26, he was released by the Cardinals and took over as Player Manager of the St. Louis Browns where he stayed until 1937.

He later came back as Manager of the Browns for part of 1952 and of the Cincinnati Reds in 1952 and 1953. As a Manager, his overall record was just 701 wins and 812 losses but, in his two years with the Cardinals, he was 153 and 116 with a pennant and World Series win and he was 141 and 116 with the Cubs in his three years with a pennant.

His career batting average of .358 is the second highest in baseball history, behind Ty Cobb, and is the best ever by a right handed hitter. He had a total of 2,930 hits in his career and his career on base percentage of .434 is the highest of any right handed batter in the history of the game. He was elected to the Baseball Hall of Fame in 1942.

Hornsby lived to play baseball. When asked what he did in the winter when there was no baseball, he said ' I'll tell you what I do. I stare out the window and wait for spring.'

He was the greatest right handed hitter in the history of the game and his performance in that six year period from 1920 to 1926 and his batting average of .424 in 1924 will probably never be equaled.

SECTION 9

Bob Gibson, of the St. Louis Cardinals, posted an Earned Run Average of 1.123 in 1968. This is the fourth best ERA ever posted for a full season and the lowest single season ERA posted since 1919. Dwight Gooden, of the New York Mets, had the second best average since 1919 with a 1.529 average in 1985.

A DIFFERENT NO HITTER

On August 31, 1993, Jim Abbott, a left handed pitcher with the New York Yankees, started a game against the Cleveland Indians in Cleveland's Municipal Stadium. He lasted just 3 2/3 innings, giving up seven runs on ten hits but, despite his dismal performance, the Yankees came back to win the game 14-8.

Five days later, facing the same Cleveland Indians, with a somewhat stronger batting lineup, in Yankee Stadium this time, Abbott pitched a no hitter and the Yankees won 4-0. The Indians had added Manny Ramirez and Jim Thome, two of the better hitters in baseball history, at designated hitter and third base, to their lineup for this game but Abbott still completely shut down the team that had bombed him five days earlier.

A no hitter is always a remarkable feat. In the entire history of baseball, there have been only 292 no hitters pitched in the 209,777 games played. Jim Abbott's no hitter is all the more remarkable because Abbott was born without a right hand and had a stump of a right arm which ended at his wrist. No pitcher in baseball history has overcome such a handicap to rise to this level.

Abbott got off to a bad start in the first inning, walking lead off batter Kenny Lofton but got a ground ball double play to erase him. He walked a batter in the second and another in the fifth but got Ramirez to hit into a double play. He walked a batter in the sixth and walked Thome with two outs in the eighth but got out of trouble each time.

He got the first two outs in the ninth and got Carlos Baerga to ground to Randy Velarde at short who threw to Don Mattingly at first for the final out in the only no hitter ever thrown by a pitcher with type handicap.

Abbott was able to balance his glove on the stump of his right arm while throwing the ball and, as soon as the ball was released, he switched the glove to under his left arm in time to field balls hit back to him. He was so amazingly quick with it that, even though teams tried to bunt to take advantage of his handicap they were not successful. In his career, he handled 381 chances fielding, had 300 assists and made just 9 errors.

He was born in Flint, Michigan, on September 9, 1967, and, despite his handicap, was an outstanding high school quarterback on the football team and pitcher on the baseball team. After high school, he was drafted by the Toronto Blue Jays in the 36th round of the 1985 Amateur Draft but opted to go to the University of Michigan instead of signing.

At Michigan, he led the baseball team to two Big Ten Championships and, in 1988, was named the Big Ten Athlete of the Year. He played in and was the country's Flag Bearer in the Pan American Games in 1987 when the United States finished second. In 1988, when baseball was demonstration sport not an official competition in the Olympics, he pitched the last game as the United States won the Gold Medal.

In 1988, he was drafted by the California Angels in the first round of the draft and signed with them on August 3, 1988. He made his Major League debut the next year on April 8, 1989 and lost to Seattle giving up three runs on six hits in 4 2/3 innings.

As a rookie, he won 12 and lost 12 with a 3.92 ERA in 29 starts. The Angels finished in third place in the seven team Western Division of the American League that year. In 1990, he slipped to 10-14 with a 4.51 ERA but started 33 games as the Angels fell to fourth at 80-82.

He had his best year with California in 1991, winning 18 and losing 11 and compiling a 2.89 ERA while throwing 5 complete games and finishing third in the Cy Young voting. The Angels fell to seventh place that year despite his performance.

In 1992, he slipped to 7-15 although his ERA in 29 starts was even lower at 2.77 and the Angels finished fifth, eighteen games under .500. At the end of the season, he was traded to the New York Yankees for three players. The Yankees finished second that year and Abbott was 11-14 with a 4.33 ERA in 33 starts. The no hitter on September 4 was, of course, the highlight of his year.

In 1994, the year of the abbreviated season, when the season ended on August 11 due to the breakdown of contract negotiations, Abbott got off to a good start. He was 9-8 in 24 starts with a 4.55 ERA when the season ended. The Yankees were in first place and this was as close as Abbott would get to playing in the post season. Because of the work stoppage, there were no playoffs that year.

At the end of the 1994 season, he became a Free Agent and, on April 8, 1995, was signed by the Chicago White Sox. He went 6-4 in 17 starts and had a 3.36 ERA before being traded back to the Angels on July 27. He won 5 and lost 4 with a 4.15 ERA with the Angels the rest of 1995.

In 1996, the Angels last year as the California Angels before becoming the Anaheim Angels, they finished in last place in the now four team Western Division and Abbott won only two games while losing 18 with a 7.48 ERA. On March 31, 1997, he was released by the Angels and did not play that year.

The Chicago White Sox signed him as a Free Agent on May 27, 1998, and he pitched at A, A+, AA, and AAA in the minors until being brought up in September. In the month of September, he won five games while losing none in five starts with a 4.55 ERA.

After the 1998 season he became a Free Agent again and was signed by the Milwaukee Brewers. With the Brewers in 1999, he won two and lost eight in 15 starts and had a 6.91 ERA. He was released by the Brewers on July 23 after pitching his last game on July 21. In that game, he came in in relief in the ninth with the Brewers down 4-0 and gave up three runs on four hits and two walks in the one inning.

Abbott overcame a tremendous handicap to make it to the Major Leagues and, even though he lost 108 games in his career, he still won 87 and pitched a no hitter for the great New York Yankees. He also pitched a total of 31 complete games in his career, a number not many pitchers in his era ever reached.

The story of Jim Abbott and how he overcame his handicap and fulfilled his dream of becoming a Major League baseball player is told in his memoir, 'Imperfect: An Improbable Life'. He now gives motivational speeches and devotes much of his time to helping others with disabilities.

His web site can be found at www.jimabbott.net and at the top of the home page the quote sums up the key to his success. It says 'Find something that you love, go after it, with all your heart.'

The Yankees' Ed 'Whitey' Ford holds the record for the most career victories by a pitcher in the World Series with 10. Yankees Red Ruffing and Allie Reynolds and St. Louis Cardinal Bob Gibson are tied for the second most with 7 each.

THE SHOT HEARD 'ROUND THE WORLD

The 1951 National League pennant race had appeared to be over on August 10, as the Dodgers had built a 12 ½ game lead over the second place New York Giants and a 14 ½ game lead over the third place Philadelphia Phillies. The Giants however would win 37 of their last 44 games but were still 4 ½ games behind on September 20. The Giants had only seven games left at that point and the Dodgers ten.

The Dodgers lost six of their last ten, while the Giants were winning all of their last seven. They were tied for first place on the last day of the season, September 30, with identical 95-58 records. The Giants beat the Boston Braves, in Boston, 3-2, on that last day and the Dodgers got a win in 14 innings against the Philadelphia Phillies, in Philadelphia so they ended the season tied at 96-58.

National League rules at the time required a three game playoff to determine the winner of the pennant in the event of a tie. The Giants and Dodgers would face each other in the playoff, beginning the next day.

Game 1 was played in the Dodgers home field, Ebbets Field, and 30,707 fans were on hand for a pitchers' duel between Brooklyn's Ralph Branca, 13-11 during the regular season and New York's Jim Hearn, 17-9.

The Dodgers got off to a 1-0 lead when left fielder Andy Pafko homered to left center in the bottom of the second. The Giants came back with two in the top of the fourth. Left fielder Monte

Irvin walked and third baseman Bobby Thomson homered to make it 2-1. In the top of the eighth Irvin homered to make it 3-1, Giants, and that was the scoring for the day. Hearn walked a batter in both the eighth and ninth but the Giants came up with double plays in each inning to preserve his complete game win. He gave up just five hits while holding the Dodgers to the one run.

The scene shifted to the Polo Grounds for Game 2 with Clem Labine on the mound for the Dodgers and Sheldon Jones for the Giants. Labine had been 5-1 in the regular season and Jones 6-11.

In the top of the first, Dodger short stop, Pee Wee Reese, singled to left and second baseman, Jackie Robinson homered to make it 2-0. The Dodgers made it 3-0 in the top of the fifth when Snider doubled to left and Robinson singled up the middle to score him.

First baseman Gil Hodges led off the sixth with a homer. Third baseman Billy Cox reached second on a throwing error by Thomson and scored on an errant throw by pitcher George Spencer who had relieved Jones. Spencer then walked Labine and Reese singled to right. Center fielder, Duke Snider, then singled in Labine to make it 6-0. In the seventh, Pafko met the Giants new pitcher, Al Corwin, with a lead off home run, his second homer of the series. Hodges then walked, catcher Rube Walker singled to center and Hodges scored when Willie Mays mishandled the ball in center, making it 8-0.

In the ninth, the Dodgers added two on a walk to Cox and a homer by Walker, to make the final 10-0 and take the series to a third game. Labine went the route for the Dodgers for the win, giving up just six hits and no runs and retiring the last ten batters in order.

Game 3, featured the Dodgers Don Newcombe, the big right hander, who had been 20-9 during the season with a 3.28 ERA and 18 complete games against the Giants Sal, The Barber, Maglie, who was 23-6 with an ERA of 2.93 and 22 complete games. The game was played at the Polo Grounds with 34,320 fans in the stands.

The Dodgers got off to a quick lead when Maglie walked Reese and Snider in the first and Robinson drove in Reese with a single to left to make it 1-0 right out of the gate. In the Giants second, after Lockman singled to left with one out, Thomson singled to left but was thrown out trying to stretch the hit into a double, to end that rally. The Giants tied it in the seventh when Irvin doubled to left, was sacrificed to third by Lockman and Thomson hit a sacrifice fly to center to make it 1-1.

In the top of the eighth, with one out, Reese and Snider got back to back singles to left to put runners on first and third. Reese scored on a wild pitch to make it 2-1. Robinson then was walked intentionally and Pafko got in infield single to score Snider. After the second out, Cox singled to left to score Robinson and it was 4-1 Dodgers. Newcombe got the Giants in order in the bottom of the eighth.

Giants Manager Leo Durocher brought in Larry Jansen, who had been 23-11 during the season, to relieve Maglie and he got the Dodgers in order in the top of the ninth and the game went to the last of the ninth, 4-1, Dodgers.

In the last of the ninth, Giants short stop Alvin Dark led off with a single to right and right fielder Don Mueller also singled to right. After Irvin fouled out to Hodges at first, Lockman doubled to left center, scoring Dark and putting runners at second and third with one out and the score 4-2, Dodgers, with Bobby Thomson coming to the plate.

The Dodgers had Carl Erskine, who had been 16-12 during the season and Ralph Branca, who had lost Game 1, pitching eight innings two days before, warming up in the bull pen. Manager Chuch Dressen elected to bring in Branca to pitch to Thomson, who had homered against him in Game 1. Branca's first pitch was a ball. Thomson hit Branca's second pitch into the left field seats, scoring Clint Hartung, who had run for Mueller, and Lockman ahead of him, and the Giants had won 5-4 and would go to the World Series.

The home run, called the 'most famous home run in baseball history' by Mike Lupica of the New York Daily News, was almost immediately dubbed 'The shot heard 'round the world' as this game was the first nationally televised sporting event ever. The Giants come from behind season was termed the Miracle of Coogan's Bluff.

The Giants would face the New York Yankees in the World Series. After going ahead two games to one, with the next two games at home, the Giants lost three in a row to drop the Series four games to two. The win was the Yankees second of what would be an unprecedented five World Series wins in a row for the Yankees.

Thomson and Branca remained close friends over the years, often appearing on television, benefits and other events together until Thomson passed away in 2010. Thomson was born in Scotland and has been inducted into the Scottish Sports Hall of Fame.

SECTION 11

Johnny Vandermeer of the Cincinnati Reds pitched a no hitter against the Boston Bees on June 11, 1938 and no hit the Brooklyn Dodgers in his next appearance, four days later, on June 15, to become the only pitcher in baseball history to throw no hitters in consecutive appearances.

THE CATCHING MOLINAS

Much has been written about the three DiMaggio brothers, Joe, Dom and Vince, all of whom played Major League baseball and all of whom played the same position, center field. There have been many other sets of brothers who have played the game but the catching Molina Brothers are unique.

Benjie, Jose and Yadier Molina all have had very successful careers in the most difficult of all positions, catcher. They were born in Puerto Rico, Benjie in 1974, Jose in 1975 and Yadier in 1982. Benjie debuted with the Los Angeles Angels on September 21, 1998, Jose with the Chicago Cubs on September 6, 1999 and Yadier with the St. Louis Cardinals on June 3, 2004.

Yadier, the most successful of the brothers is still, as of this writing, catching for the Cardinals and is still, arguably, the best defensive catcher in baseball.

He has been with the Cardinals his entire 12 year career and has a career batting average of .286. He has been named to the All Star team in each of the last seven years and has played in four World Series, losing against the Red Sox in 2004 and 2013 and winning against the Tigers in 2006 and the Rangers in 2011. He has always been a clutch hitter and, in his four World Series appearances, he has batted .328, with 22 hits in 67 at bats in 21 games. Similarly, in six National League Championship series appearances he has averaged .325, well above his more than respectable .286 lifetime career average.

He has won the Gold Glove as the best defensive National League catcher every year for the last eight years and the Platinum Glove Award for the best overall defensive player in the league four times in the last five years. The only National League catcher to win the Gold Glove more times was Cincinnati's great Hall of Famer, Johnny Bench, who won it 10 times.

He is an iron man among catchers, catching an average of 126 games a year for his career. He has thrown out 44 percent of all runners who have attempted to steal a base against him, well above the Major League average of 28 percent during his career.

The oldest, Benjie, eight years older than Yadier, caught in the major leagues from 1998 until 2010, spending seven years with the Anaheim Angels, who became the Los Angeles Angels of Anaheim, from 1998-2005, the Toronto Blue Jays in 2006, the San Francisco Giants from 2007-2010 and finished his career in 2010 with the Texas Rangers after being traded in mid season from San Francisco. Ironically, with San Francisco playing Texas in the World Series that year, and Benjie playing for Texas, he would have gotten a world series ring no matter who won as he had played for both teams that year.

He was also with the Angels when they won the World Series in 2002 and hit .286 in that series. Benjie had a career lifetime average of .274 in 1,362 games and hit 144 homers and had 711 RBI's.

Middle brother, Jose, who caught for the Tampa Bay Rays until 2014, was a fine defensive catcher like his younger brother and known for his ability to handle young pitchers. He is one year younger than Benjie and was drafted by the Chicago Cubs in 1993 in the 14th round of the draft. He made his debut with the Cubs on September 6, 1999 but spent most of the next three years in the minors.

In 2001, he went to the Anaheim Angels and was there until 2007. From 2002 through 2005, he and Benjie shared catching duties with the Angels with Benjie getting the bulk of the work. Jose spent 2007-2009 with the Yankees and 2010-2011 with the Toronto Blue Jays before going to Tampa Bay where he played until 2014.

Jose had only averaged 56 games played per year before going to Tampa, where he caught 102 games in 2012, 99 in 2013 and 80 in 2014. He had a lifetime average of .234 and hit just 39 homers and drove in 213 runs in his career. Like his younger brother Yadier, Jose was adept at throwing out runners stealing, cutting down 37 per cent in his career.

He played in the World Series with the Angels in 2002 when they beat the San Francisco Giants and with the Yankees in 2009 when they beat the Philadelphia Phillies.

The Molina brothers are unique. Between them, the three have caught 3,636 major league baseball games. Yadier has had, by far, the most successful career of the three. He is one of the top catchers in the game today.

Financially, they have all done well. Jose made $2.75 million in his last year, his best year financially, while Benjie made $6.5 million with San Francisco in 2009 and little brother Yadier is under contract to St. Louis through 2018 at $15. million per year.

Baseball has been good to the Molina brothers but they have also been good to baseball. There has been a Molina in the World Series in seven of the last fourteen years and Yadier could end up there again before his career is over.

SECTION 12

Ken Griffey, Jr., was elected to the Hall of Fame in 2016 with the highest percentage of votes ever recorded. He was named on 99.3 percent of the ballots topping the previous high of 98.84 for Tom Seaver in 1992.

THE 1975 WORLD SERIES

The 1975 World Series matched the Cincinnati Reds, who had not won a World Series in 34 years, with the Boston Red Sox, who had not won one in 57 years. The Reds had been to the series in 1970 and 1972 but had been beaten both times. The Sox had last been to the series in 1967 and lost.

Rookie Red Sox center fielder Fred Lynn who won the Most Valuable Player and Rookie of the year awards in the American League was joined by such stars as Carl Yazstremski, Dwight Evans, Carlton Fisk and Luis Tiant. Jim Rice, who had finished second in the Rookie of the Year voting and third in the MVP voting, did not play in the series due to an injured wrist.

The Reds, known as the Big Red Machine in those years and led by National League MVP, Joe Morgan, also had Johnny bench, who finished fourth in the MVP voting and Pete Rose who had finished fifth.

The Series opened up in Boston's Fenway Park on October 11. Luis Tiant and Don Gullett were wrapped up in a 0-0 duel for six innings of Game 1 and Tiant held the Reds scoreless in the top of the seventh.

In the bottom of the seventh, Tiant led off with a single to left field. Dwight Evans then attempted a sacrifice bunt and, when the Reds tried to get Tiant at second, both runners were safe. Denny Doyle then singled to left to load the bases and Carl Yastrzemski singled to left to score Tiant and leave the bases loaded.

Clay Carroll replaced Reds starter Don Gullett and walked Fisk to force in Evans with the second run. Will McEnaney was brought in to pitch and struck out Fred Lynn swinging. Rico Petrocelli then singled to left to score Doyle and Yaz and it was 4-0. Rick Burleson singled to right to score Fisk and Cecil Cooper hit a sacrifice fly to score Petrocelli and it was 6-0.

It stayed that way the rest of the way as Tiant went the route, giving up just five hits and getting the complete game shut out.

In Game 2, the Sox got one in the first when Fisk singled to drive in Yaz. Yaz had hit into a ground ball force at second and, when Cooper who had doubled and was on third, tried to score, he was caught in a rundown and Yaz ended up on second. Joe Morgan scored in the fourth on a fielder's choice to make it 1-1. In the sixth, Petrocelli drove in Yaz with a single to left to make it 2-1, Boston.

In the ninth Bench doubled to left, to lead off and Dick Drago replaced starter Bill Lee and got the next two batters. With the Reds down to their last out Dave Concepcion got an infield single to score Bench and Ken Griffey doubled to left to score him and make it 3-2, Reds. Rawley Eastwick, who had pitched a scoreless eighth, got the Sox in order in the ninth and the series went to Cincinnati tied one game each.

The Reds won Game 3, at Riverfront Stadium, 6-5, in ten innings. The Sox scored first on a solo homer by Fisk in the second but Bench hit a two run homer to put the Reds up 2-1 in the fourth. In the fifth, the Reds got three on homers by Concepcion and Geronimo, a triple by Pete Rose and a sac fly by Morgan.

The Sox chipped away when Yaz scored on a sacrifice fly in the sixth and Carbo hit a pinch hit homer in the seventh. In the top of the ninth, Evans tied it at 5-5 with a two run homer. In the bottom of the tenth Morgan singled in Geronimo with the winning run and it was two games to one in favor of the Reds.

Despite giving up two runs in the first and two more in the fourth, Luis Tiant pitched his second complete game win in Game 4. The Sox got five in the top of the fourth to go up 5-2. Fisk and Lynn singled to start the inning and, with one out, Evans tripled to right to drive them in and Burleson doubled to left to score Evans.

Tiant then got a ground ball single moving Burleson to third and Beniquez reached on an error and Burleson scored and Tiant went to second. Yaz then singled to right to score Tiant with what turned out to be the winning run. Not only had Tiant pitched two complete game wins, he also scored what turned out to be the winning run in both games. He gave up two runs in the fourth but shut the Reds down the rest of the way and the series was tied at two games each.

In Game 5, Reggie Cleveland started for the Sox and gave up two homers to Perez, a solo blast in the fourth and a three run homer in the sixth as the Reds won easily 6-2 to go up three games to two going back to Boston.

Don Gullett started for the Reds and gave up a run in the first but shut out the Sox until the top of the ninth when, with two outs, Yaz singled to right center and Fisk lined a single to left. Lynn then doubled down the right field line, scoring Yaz and sending Fisk to third. Rawly Eastwick came in to relieve Gullett and struck out Petrocelli swinging to end the game at 6-2, Reds. The series would go back to Fenway with the Reds up three games to two.

After three days of rain postponed Game 6, Tiant started Game 6 and gave up five runs to trail 5-3 going into the eighth. He gave up a solo homer to Geronimo to lead off the eighth to make it 6-3 and was removed.

In the bottom of the eighth, Bernie Carbo hit his second pinch hit homer of the series with Lynn and Petrocelli on to tie the game at 6-6 and set up one of the most memorable finishes in World

Series history.

In the bottom of the twelfth, Fisk, leading off, hit a long fly down the left field line that just stayed fair for the winning homer. The picture of Fisk trying to wave the ball fair as he began to run to first is one of the most viewed pictures in Red Sox and baseball history.

The final game went to the top of the ninth tied 3-3. The Sox had gotten three in the third on an RBI single by Yaz and then, after Fisk was walked intentionally to load the bases, Petrocelli and Evans walked, forcing in two more runs.

Perez hit a homer to make it 3-2 in the sixth and Rose drove in Griffey with the tying run in the seventh. In the top of the ninth, with Griffey on second after walking again, Morgan drove him in with what turned out to be the winning run.

Pete Rose, who hit .370, with 10 hits in 27 at bats, was named MVP. Five players who played in the series, Johnny Bench, Joe Morgan and Tony Perez from the Reds and Carlton Fisk and Carl Yastrzemski from the Sox, were later named to the Hall of Fame.

The Sox had come so close but would not win a series until 2004. It was one of the most exciting and suspense filled series ever with five of the seven games decided by one run.

Fenway Park, in Boston, home of the Red Sox, built in 1912 is the oldest ballpark still in use in Major League Baseball. Wrigley Field in Chicago, home of the Cubs, is the second oldest, built in 1914 two years after Fenway.

CAPTAIN CARL YASTRZEMSKI

On September 12, 1979, Carl Yastrzemski got his 3,000[th] Major League hit. He did it, at age 40, while batting third in the Sox lineup, against the New York Yankees in a game the Red Sox won, 9-2. Yaz would go on to get another 419 hits before ending his career on October 2, 1983, at age 44.

He was born, August 22, 1939, in Southhampton, NY, and was an outstanding athlete in High School. He was given a scholarship to Notre Dame University after High School to play both baseball and basketball. However, his talent in baseball was so impressive that he was signed by the Red Sox in 1958, during his first year at Notre Dame.

He was sent to Raleigh in the Carolina League his first year, 1959, and hit .377, winning the Most Valuable Player and Rookie of the Year Awards in the league. The next year, 1960, he was promoted to Minneapolis in the AAA American Association where he hit .339.

He was brought up and played his first game for the Red Sox on opening day of the 1961 season. He started in left field and batted fifth between Jackie Jensen, the right fielder, and Pete Runnels, the third baseman. Runnels had won the batting title in 1960 and would win it again in 1962. Yaz's first time up, he singled to left field but went one for five for the day as the Sox lost, 5-2.

In Game number two of the season and his career, the Sox beat the California Angels 3-0 and Yaz drove in two of the runs and scored the third. In the first inning, he singled to center to drive in second baseman Chuck Schilling with the game's first run. In the third, he tripled to center and scored on Runnels double and, in the fifth he hit a sacrifice fly to left to score center fielder Gary Geiger with the third run.

If there ever was a sign that a great player had arrived, that game was it. He went on to hit just .266 that first year but improved to .296 in 1962 and to .321 in 1963 when he won the first of his three American League batting titles.

In 1967, the Year of the Impossible Dream, Yaz had a spectacular year. The Sox had finished ninth of ten teams in the American League in 1966, and were not expected to do any better in 1967. They had won just 72 and lost 90 in 1966, finishing ninth in the then ten team American League, 1 ½ games ahead of the last place Yankees and attendance was only 811,172 at home.

In 1967, they turned the record around and won 92 while losing 70 to win the American League pennant and attendance improved to 1,727,832. There were many heroes that year but no one did more to propel that team from ninth to first than Carl Yastrzemski.

Yaz hit .326 to win the American League batting title. He drove in 121 runs, the most in the league, and hit 44 homers to tie Harmon Killebrew for the most homers. He won the Triple Crown, the second Sox player in history to do so. Ted Williams had won it in 1942 and 1947 and no one would win it again until Miguel Cabrera of the Detroit Tigers did in 2012, 45 years later. Yaz was also named Most Valuable Player and Baseball's Player of the Year.

The American League season that year came down the final weekend before being decided. The Sox had to sweep the Minnesota Twins who were in first by one game and the Detroit Tigers had to lose one of their last two games against the Angels for the Sox to win the pennant.

Yaz went seven for eight in those two games with a homer and six RBI's. In Game 1, he put the Sox ahead, 2-1, with an RBI single in the fifth and, with the score 3-2, Boston, in the seventh, he put the icing on the cake with a three run homer to put the game out of reach as the Sox won 6-4. In Game 2, he went four for four with three singles and a double and his single with the bases loaded in the sixth drove in two to tie the game at 2-2. The Sox got three more in that inning, including one scored by Yaz, to make it 5-2 and went on to win 5-3.

The win assured the Sox of at least a tie for the pennant at 92-70 but the Tigers who were still 91-70 were playing their last game against California.

Pandemonium broke loose in Fenway at the end of the game and the fans took to the field to celebrate, ripping up sod and taking any souvenir they could of the game. I was in the ball park that day and in traffic after the crowd had cleared out of Fenway. When the radio announced that the Tigers lead off hitter, Dick McAuliffe had hit into a double play to end the game and the Tigers had lost giving the Red Sox the pennant, it seemed like every car horn in Boston blew.

In the World Series against the St. Louis Cardinals which the Sox lost in seven games, Yaz went 10 for 25 at the plate, a .400 average, with three homers, two doubles, five RBI's and four runs scored.

He only played in one other post season, 1975, when the Sox swept the American League Championship Series against Oakland and lost in seven games to the Cincinnati Reds in the Series. He went 5-11 in the Playoff and 9-29 in the World Series. In his post season play, including two World Series appearances, he hit .369 with 24 hits in 65 at bats.

His career batting average was .285 and he had 452 homers among his 3,419 hits. In his 23 years with the Red Sox, he made 13,992 plate appearances, more than any other player in baseball history beside Pete Rose. He was named to 18 All Star teams and played his entire 23 year career for the Red Sox. He was elected to the Hall of Fame in 1989 with 94.6 % of the vote.

Yaz got his last hit, 22 years and four months after his first, in the final game of the 1983 season, on October 2, against the Cleveland Indians. He singled with two out in the third off Cleveland starter Bud Anderson and retired at the end of the season.

Captain Carl was one of the greatest players in Red Sox history and the year he had in 1967 was one of the greatest any player has ever had in baseball history.

Ricky Henderson has scored the most runs in baseball history with 2,295. Ty Cobb, with 2,244, is second, and Barry Bonds third, with 2,227. Babe Ruth and Henry Aaron are tied for fourth with 2,174.

BOB GIBSON

We live in an era where starting pitchers are only expected to get through six innings and they have done their job. Every major league team has middle relievers, a set up man or men and a closer who are expected to finish the job the starter began.

In 1968, Bob Gibson, who, by the way, was 6'2" and weighed 190 pounds, small by today's standards but big for his time, won 22 games and lost 9. He pitched 28 complete games out of 34 starts. To put that 28 complete games in perspective, the 2015 Cleveland Indians entire team led the Majors in complete games with 11 and the average number of complete games per TEAM that year was 3.47.

In addition, he had 13 complete game shutouts and pitched a total of 304.2 innings. Most pitchers don't throw more than 180 innings a year today. His earned run average for the season was a phenomenal 1.12, the fourth lowest in the history of baseball and the lowest ERA recorded since 1914. He had 268 strikeouts in his 304+ innings. He won the Cy Young Award and the National League's Most Valuable Player award.

If those numbers are not enough to stagger your mind, think about this. From April 26 until May 6 of that year, a period of ten days, Gibson pitched 32 innings, gave up 2 earned runs and won three games. This unbelievable stretch started on April 26 with a complete nine inning game against the Pittsburgh Pirates in which he gave up one earned run.

On May 1, he pitched a complete game in a win over Houston in which he threw TWELVE innings without giving up an earned run. He followed this up five days later by pitching an ELEVEN inning complete game against the New York Mets while giving up just one earned run.

In the period from June 3 through July 29 of that year, he pitched 90 innings and gave up a total of 2 runs for an earned run average of 0.20. During that stretch, he won 10 games without a loss and pitched complete games of nine innings in every one of those ten starts.

He pitched his team to the World Series where they met the Detroit Tigers that year. In the first game of the series, he struck out a world series record 17 batters and pitched a complete game shutout against the best the American League had. In game 4, he pitched another complete game, this time a 5 hitter, to give his team a 3-1 series lead. He came back on two days rest and pitched game number 7 but lost the game and the series 4-1.

That was Gibson's third World Series. In the 1964 Series, against the New York Yankees, he had won two games and lost one as his team won the Series. He pitched eight innings in Game 2 as the Cardinals lost 8-3. He came back with a 10 inning complete game in Game 5 to beat the Yankees 5-2 and threw another complete game in Game 7, beating the Yankees for the Championship 7-5. He had pitched 27 innings in eight days and given up just nine runs. He was named Most Valuable Player of the Series.

In 1967, the Cards faced the Boston Red Sox in the Series. All Gibson did was pitch complete games in Games 1, 4 and 7, winning all three as the Cards beat the Sox four games to three. In Game 1, he held the Sox to six hits and won 2-1. In Game 4, he pitched a five hit shutout as the Cards won 6-0. In Game 7, he gave up just three hits and two runs as the Cards won the game, 7-2, and the Series four games to three. He was named Most Valuable Player of the Series, again.

In three World Series, Gibson started nine games and finished eight of them. He won seven and lost 2 and had an ERA of 1.89. If there was ever a Big Game Pitcher, Bob Gibson was it.

In his career, he won 251 games and lost 174 and had an ERA of 2.91 over 3,884+ innings. He won the Cy Young Award in 1968 and 1970, was named to the All Star Team nine times and won the Gold Glove nine times. He was elected to the Hall of Fame in 1981 with 84% of the vote.

Born on November 9, 1935, in Omaha, Nebraska, he was signed by the St. Louis Cardinals as a Free Agent in 1957 and made his Major League debut with the Cardinals on April 15, 1959. He played with the Cardinals his entire career, from 1959 until 1975.

Bob Gibson has been called the most intimidating pitcher in baseball history. He was a dominating figure in the game for many years up there with Sandy Koufax, Cy Young, Bob Feller, Nolan Ryan and all the rest of the best of the best. I doubt very much if anyone of the others, as great as they were, ever had a more successful season than he did in 1968 and I am sure that no one will ever have another one that even approaches it.

In 1975, Fred Lynn of the Boston Red Sox, helped lead the Sox to the American League Pennant, hitting .331 with 21 homers and 105 RBI's. He was named American League Rookie of the Year and Most Valuable Player, the first person in baseball history to receive both those honors in the same year.

THE AMERICAN DREAM, BASEBALL STYLE

Imagine this version of the American Dream. A young man graduates from High School in the west and goes on to a University where he tries out for the baseball team. Just out of high school, at 5'8', 135 pounds, he doesn't make the team so he takes the position as Team Manager because baseball is his dream and he wants to be around it.

A Manager in college baseball is not the same as Manager in Professional Ball. The College Baseball Manager is the go-fer that takes care of equipment and is a glorified errand boy for the real players.

During the next two years, while going to school and performing his duties as Manager, he works out as much as he can and plays as much baseball as he can trying to hone those skills so that he can someday play at a higher level.

After his second year at college, he transfers to a nearby Junior College, where he not only makes the team but is named a Junior College All American his first year. The college where he originally started gives him a baseball scholarship to return for his senior year. That year, he hits .395 and is named to the first team All West Coast Conference Team.

Even after two very impressive years in college ball, he is not drafted by any major league team so he joins an Independent League team playing in the west. Finally, in 2008, a major league team notices him and purchases the rights to him from the Independent League Team for one dollar.

He is sent to the minor leagues where he hits well and progresses quickly through the organization's farm system for the next two years.

Fast forward to June 12, 2010. Our young man makes his debut in Major League baseball. In his first at bat he hits the first pitch he has ever seen in the big leagues for a grand slam home run. He gets into 60 Major League games that year, batting .242 with 39 hits in 161 at bats. The home run he hit in his first at bat is the only homer he hits all year.

In 2011, he spends the year in AAA, hitting .268 with 10 homers and 48 RBI's. In 2012, he shuttles back and forth from AAA to the Majors and, in just 88 games in the big leagues, he hits .243, with six homers and 33 RBI's.

At the start of the 2013 season, he makes the big league team, ends up playing in 134 games, hitting .303 with 12 homers and 66 RBI's. He plays the outfield and even fills in at first base as needed. His team surprises everyone and wins its division title, then goes on the win the league championship and, eventually, the World Series.

Our hero, who couldn't make his college team 13 years ago, is now the proud owner of a World Series ring, the most coveted prize in the baseball world. That was the story of Daniel Nava, a young man who made his dream come true with the Boston Red Sox through hard work and perseverance.

The story doesn't end there, though. The next year, the team fell apart and finished in last place but he still hit .270 in 113 games. The following year, he is caught up in and maybe even a victim of bad management that finds his team with eight major league outfielders and not enough pitching as the season starts. He ends up being sent back to the minors while the other, more expensive mistakes that his team has made battle for spots in the lineup while the team sinks lower and lower into the basement of the division.

Eventually, in 2015, after hitting .250 in 10 games in the minors and only .152 in 66 games in Boston, he was designated for assignment. The Sox placed him on waivers and, on August 5, he was claimed off waivers by the Tampa Bay Rays. He played in 31 games for the Rays the rest of the season, playing the outfield and first base and hit just .233 with 17 hits in 73 at bats. On November 25, 2015, he was granted Free Agency.

The Los Angeles Angels of Anaheim signed him to a one year contract for $1.375 million dollars on December 16, 2015 and, as of this writing, he was expected to platoon in left field with Craig Gentry.

Daniel Nava will be 33 years old when the 2016 season starts. He will never make the Hall of Fame and will never be named as one of the best 100 players of all time. He will probably never even get enough Big League time to qualify for a pension.

The story of his brief career in baseball history is not the stuff that young boys and men usually think about when they aspire to a professional baseball career. It is, however, another example of the American Dream where a young man, of limited ability, through hard work, discipline and desire forces his way to the top.

Not many people who could not make their college team have played on a team that won a World Series and have the ring to prove it but Daniel Nava's journey provides inspiration not only for aspiring ball players but for young people with a dream everywhere.

Hank Aaron holds the record for most career extra base hits with a total of 1,477. Barry Bonds is second with 1440 and Stan Musial third with 1,377. Babe Ruth and Willie Mays have the fourth and fifth highest totals. Alex Rodriguez, sixth, with 1,259 and Albert Pujols, eleventh, with 1,159 are the only active players in the top twelve.

SANDY KOUFAX

On September 11, 1966, Dodger left hander, Sandy Koufax, pitched the last complete game shut out of his career. That day, he held the Houston Astros to six hits while striking out six and walking two. It was the last of his 40 complete game shut outs in his injury shortened 12 year career, however, it was not the last of his 137 complete games.

From that day until the end of the season, and his career, Koufax pitched five more complete games giving him six complete games in 22 days. In those last six games of his career, he won five and lost one, striking out 45 batters and giving up just six earned runs for an earned run average of 1.02.

A complete game shutout is pretty big news today in baseball. For Koufax, it was just business as usual. After all, he threw 27 complete games and 5 shutouts that year. The year before, he pitched 27 complete games and had eight shut outs. In the two year period, of 82 games he started, he finished 54.

To put those numbers in perspective, the six pitchers who tied for the lead for the most complete games pitched in all of baseball in 2015, with four games each, had less complete games between them than Koufax had in either of those years. In the four year span from 1963-1966, Koufax threw 89 complete games including 31 complete game shutouts.

Sandy Koufax pitched for the Dodgers from 1955 until 1966, when, at age 30, he was forced to retire because of traumatic arthritis in his elbow which threatened a permanent disability if he did not. He is believed by many to have been the greatest pitcher the game has ever seen.

From 1963 until 1966, the last four years of his career, he won an amazing 97 games while losing just 27. During that four year period, he had a total earned run average of 1.86, led the league in ERA each year, and won the Cy Young Award 3 times, 1963, 1965 and 1966. He was named MVP in the National League in 1963 and MVP in the World Series in 1963 and 1965.

He threw 1192 2/3 innings during the regular season those four years, striking out 1,228 batters, 382 in 1965, and started 41 games in each of his last 2 seasons, 150 over the 4 year period. His total of 382 strikeouts in 1965 was only exceeded in the Modern Era by Nolan Ryan's 383 in 1973.

In 1963, after Koufax won 25 and lost 5, Yogi Berra, according to the baseball Hall of Fame, said ' I can see how he won 25 games. What I don't understand is how he lost 5.'

Forced to retire at 30, in his prime, one can only imagine what his final totals would have been. He won 53 and lost just 17 in his last two years and won 165 and lost 87 for his 12 year career.

Born in Brooklyn, New York, he attended Lafayette High School there and went on to the University of Cincinnati where he earned a basketball scholarship as a walk on. He also played baseball there and was signed by the Dodgers in 1954. His first year with the Dodgers his salary, according to Bill James' Historical Abstract, was $6,000. The most he made in his career was $125,000. in 1966, his last year.

His first 8 years in the majors, he had control problems and until he overcame those problems, he won just 68 and lost 60. He was a hard throwing left handed pitcher who was 6'2" tall and weighed 210 pounds. As a rookie, in 1955, there was no question about his velocity but control was a problem. Dodger Great Duke Snyder, Koufax's Hall of Fame teammate once said, 'When he first came up he couldn't throw a ball inside the batting cage.

In the 1965 World Series, against the Minnesota Twins, which the Dodgers won 4 games to 3, Koufax was named the MVP. After taking the loss in Game 1, although he went six innings, giving up just 1 earned run and striking out 9, he came back and shut the Twins out in games 5 and 7. On October 11, he gave up just four hits while going the route and, just three days later, gave up only three hits for his second straight complete game shutout and the World Championship.

In that series, he threw 24 innings, struck out 29 batters, and gave up just 1 earned run for an ERA of 0.38. In his post season career, he pitched in 4 World Series, appearing in 8 games, striking out 61 while walking just 11 and posting an ERA of 0.95.

He made his debut with the then Brooklyn Dodgers on June 24, 1955 and threw his last game on October 2, 1966 with the transplanted Los Angeles Dodgers. In 1972, he was elected to the Baseball Hall of Fame, at age 36 years and 20 days, the youngest player ever elected to the Hall.

He was the first major league pitcher to throw four no hitters including a perfect game on September 9, 1965. He was on four World Series winning teams in 1955, 1959, 1963 and 1965 and on 7 All Star teams.

Sandy Koufax did it all in a very short career. If not for the arthritis that forced him to retire at age 30, in his prime and seemingly getting better and better, there is no telling how many games he would have won. No wonder, at age 80, he is still a fixture in the Dodgers organization and still works with young pitchers in spring training.

SECTION 17

Don Newcombe, the Brooklyn Dodgers right handed pitcher, won the Cy Young Award in 1956, the first year of the Award. He also won the National League's Most Valuable Player Award that year, after winning 27 and losing 7 with a 3.06 ERA. The Dodgers won the pennant but lost to the Yankees in the World Series, four games to three.

FREDDY PARENT

A small percentage of Major League ballplayers come from areas with colder climates than those from warmer climates. The reason for this is very simple, people born in colder climates have a shorter season in which weather allows them to play ball outside and, hence, a shorter time to develop skills.

This is not as true as it was when professional baseball first began. High school and college teams, from colder climates such as North Dakota and Maine, were lucky to be able to fit in a 10 or 15 game schedule in the spring. Today, with school teams, including those from the colder climates, making southern swings and practicing in large indoor facilities year round, there is less of an advantage to those from warmer climates.

When I cover Spring training in Tampa, Florida, the motel that I stay at houses a high school team from northern New York state that plays a 10-15 game schedule in Florida every year.

Division I College baseball is the equivalent of another Minor League with teams playing a schedule of 50 to 60 games, not counting Fall Ball and regional, super regional and world series tournaments in late spring and early summer.

Throughout baseball history, there have been many players who overcame the disadvantage of coming from colder environments and became outstanding Major League players. Being a resident of Maine, I would be remiss if I didn't mention at least some ball players who came from Maine and other, colder climates and had outstanding professional careers.

One such player was Freddy Parent, who was born in Biddeford, Maine, and played with the St. Louis Perfectos, the Boston Americans and the Chicago White Sox in a Major League career that lasted from 1899 until 1911 and who lived in Sanford, Maine, after his playing days.

He was born Alfred Joseph Parent on November 11, 1875 and was the oldest of 10 children. Freddy left school at age 14 and at age 16 worked in a textile mill in Sanford. He played in many places in Maine and New Hampshire, including a stint with the Sanford Town Team, sponsored by the mill, before leaving Maine in 1898 to play for the New Haven Team in the Connecticut League.

In two years at New Haven, Freddy hit .326 and .349 and was brought up to the National League Perfectos for just a 2 game tryout when the Perfectos were playing the Giants in New York during the 1899 season before being sent back to New Haven.

In 1900, he played for the Providence Grays in the Eastern League where he hit .287 and was signed by the Boston Americans, now the Boston Red Sox, in 1901. Freddy was a small shortstop , even for those days, at 5'7" and 154 pounds, who batted and threw right handed. Most people felt he was too small to make a career in baseball but Freddy was committed to playing big league baseball.

He is said to have been a slick fielder and fast runner who stole 184 bases in his career. He earned the nickname 'The Flying Frenchman'. In his first year with the Americans, he hit .306 and became the club's regular shortstop.

In his first three years in the Majors, Freddy became one of the first of the Iron Men, playing in 413 consecutive games, a record at the time. These were the first 413 games ever played by what was to become the Boston Red Sox franchise.

In 1903, the American's won the American League pennant and went on to beat the Pittsburgh Pirates 5 games to 3 in the first World Series ever played. Freddy hit .304 with 17 triples, 24 stolen bases and 80 RBIs that season and then scored 8 runs and drove in 4 more while hitting .290 in the World Series. In 1904, Freddy hit .291 with 28 steals and 77 RBIs. The American's won the pennant again but there was no World Series that year. The Series was resumed the following year.

Freddy played for the Americans through the 1907 season when he went to the Chicago White Sox where he played until 1911. After hitting over .300 in 2 of his first three years in the majors, he never hit .300 again but he was a steady fielder who played hard and never played less than 138 games in a full season from 1901 through 1906. When he began playing in the major leagues a full season was 138 games before being increased to 154 when the league expanded to two 8 team leagues.

Freddy had a .262 career batting average with just 20 homers and 471 RBIs. He had the distinction in his career of getting the only hit in a game for his team to prevent a no hitter three different times and also played for the then Boston Pilgrims, behind Cy Young, in his perfect game against Connie Mack's Philadelphia Athletics and Rube Waddell on May 5, 1904. This was the first perfect game in Major League history after 1900.

After leaving the Major Leagues in 1911, Freddy joined the Baltimore Orioles who were then in the International League, as a player coach. He moved to second base and enjoyed three more productive years there, hitting .290 from age 36-38. In 1914, George Herman 'Babe' Ruth joined the Baltimore team on his way to the big leagues and fame and Freddy became his mentor.

Freddy never lost his love for and commitment to the game of baseball. After his playing days were over, he managed the

Springfield Ponies in the Eastern League in 1918 and the Lewiston Red Sox in the New England League in 1919. He coached Colby College's baseball team from 1921 – 1924 and was an Assistant Coach at Harvard from 1926 – 1928.

Freddy passed away in 1972 at the age of 96. Prior to his death, he was the last surviving participant in the first World Series of all time. Like his fellow Maine big leaguer, Pitcher Colby Jack Coombs, whose career is dealt with in another section of this book, Freddy devoted his entire life to baseball and made the cold weather State of Maine proud.

SECTION 18

In addition to having the most career home runs of any player in history, 762, Barry Bonds also received more walks, 2,558, and more intentional walks, 688, than any other player.

THE EVOLUTION OF THE MAJOR LEAGUE TEAMS

Major League Baseball is made up of two leagues, the American League and the National League. There are fifteen teams in each league, divided into three Divisions, with five teams in each Division. There are teams all over America, from the east coast to the west coast and from the northern border to the southern border and even one team, the Toronto Blue Jays, in Canada.

In 1901, when baseball was in its infancy, Major League Baseball was made up of the same two leagues but with just sixteen teams, eight in each league. The western United States was relatively new and travel was difficult in those days. As a result, the teams were based mostly in the eastern population centers, with the St. Louis Cardinals, in the National League and the Milwaukee Brewers in the American League the teams based the farthest west.

The two leagues were made up of the following teams, listed in order of their finish in the 2001 season;

AMERICAN	NATIONAL
Chicago White Sox	Pittsburgh Pirates
Boston Americans	Philadelphia Phillies
Detroit Tigers	Brooklyn Superbas
Philadelphia Athletics	St. Louis Cardinals
Baltimore Orioles	Boston Beaneaters
Washington Senators	Chicago Orphans
Cleveland Blues	New York Giants
Milwaukee Brewers	Cincinnati Reds

In 1902, the St. Louis Browns replaced the Milwaukee Brewers in the American League and the two westernmost teams were now both from St. Louis, Missouri. Also, in 1902, the Cleveland Blues changed their name to the Cleveland Bronchos.

In 1903, the New York Highlanders replaced the Baltimore Orioles in the American League and Cleveland changed their name again to the Cleveland Naps in honor of their great Manager Napoleon Lajoie. That same year, the Chicago Orphans became the Chicago Cubs.

Over the next few years there were several name changes but the franchises stayed in place. In 1907, the Boston Americans became the Red Sox and the Boston Beaneaters became the Boston Doves.

In 1911, the Brooklyn Superbas changed their name to the Dodgers but would change it to the Brooklyn Robins in 1914 and remained that until returning to the name Dodgers in 1932. The Braves briefly became the Rustlers in 1911 before adopting the name Braves in 1912.

The name changes of the Brooklyn and Boston National League teams of 1911 did not improve their fortunes as the Dodgers finished in seventh place and the Rustlers in eighth that year.

In 1913, the Highlanders became the New York Yankees and, in 1915, Cleveland adopted the name Indians.

After Brooklyn became the Dodgers again in 1932, the eight teams retained the same names and locations until 1953, except the Boston Braves, who were known as the Boston Bees from 1936 until 1940 when they reverted to the name Braves. In 1953 the Braves moved to Milwaukee and became the Milwaukee Braves.

The exodus from the original cities, and the expansion westward, started with the Braves move to Milwaukee in 1953 and was quickly followed by the St. Louis Browns moving to Baltimore, Maryland, and becoming the Orioles in 1954. The Philadelphia Athletics then moved to Kansas City where they became the Kansas City Athletics in 1955.

Three years later, in 1958, both the Dodgers and Giants made their infamous moves from New York to Los Angeles and San Francisco respectively. Over fifty years later, there is still bad feeling in New York about the teams 'desertion' of New York. The fact is that Ebbetts Field, where the Dodgers played was inadequate and the Giants had been losing money with a mediocre team playing in the old Polo Grounds and the move made good business sense.

In 1961, the American League added the Minnesota Twins and the Los Angeles Angels and, in 1962, the National League added the New York Mets and the Houston Colt 45's giving each league ten teams, all in one division.

In 1969, the Kansas City Royals and Seattle Pilots, later the Mariners, were added to the American League and the San Diego Padres and Montreal Expos were added to the National League. Both leagues then divided their twelve teams into two six team divisions, an Eastern and a Western Division.

In 1972, the Washington Senators became the Texas Rangers and the leagues remained the same with twelve teams divided into two divisions.

The Toronto Blue Jays and Seattle Mariners joined the American League in 1977 and the Florida Marlins, later to become the Miami Marlins, and the Colorado Rockies joined the National League in 1993.

In 1994, with fourteen teams in each league, the leagues were divided into three Divisions. Each Eastern and Central Division had five teams in it and each Western Division had four. Due to the work stoppage and the abbreviated season in 1994, there were no playoffs that year. In 1995, the Wild Card system was instituted and more teams were added to the playoffs.

The Arizona Diamondbacks were added in 1998 and the Montreal Expos folded and their place was taken by the Washington Nationals in 2005. From 1998 until 2012, there were sixteen teams in the National League and only fourteen in the American. In 2013, the Houston Astros were moved from the National League to the American League to balance the numbers and now each team is comprised of three, five team Divisions.

When the World Series began in 1903, the winner of each league played in the World Series. Since then a playoff system has evolved as the leagues got bigger. There is no point in trying to explain the Wild Card System in this space as, by the time I got it explained it would probably be changed, again.

As with everything else, baseball has become more and more complicated and, even though the sport keeps growing, those in charge continue to tinker with it. One of my favorite sayings is 'If it ain't broke, don't fix it' and one thing that indicates it does well on its own is the fact that, of that original sixteen franchises, almost all of them all are still a part of 'America's Pastime' one hundred and fifteen years later.

Ty Cobb was in the top ten in batting average in the league in 20 different season, the most times of any player in history, since 1903. Stan Musial was second with 17 years. Tris Speaker and Honus Wagner were tied for third with 16 years each.

DON DRYSDALE

Don Drysdale began his Major League career with the Brooklyn Dodgers on April 17, 1956. He was with them when they moved to Los Angeles in 1958 and he spent his entire 14 year career as a Dodger. Born Donald Scott Drysdale on July 23, 1936 in Los Angeles, California, he was signed by the Dodgers as a Free Agent in 1954 at the age of 17.

He was 8-5 that year in C ball at Bakersfield, California and, in 1955, he moved quickly to AAA at Montreal in the International League where he was 11-11 with a 3.33 ERA.

The next year, in his first year in the Majors, he won five and lost five with a 2.64 ERA. In his first start in the Majors, he pitched a complete game against the Phillies in Philadelphia, giving up one run on nine hits and winning 6-1.

The Dodgers won the National League pennant that year and lost to the Yankees in the World Series, four games to three. Drysdale got into one game in the series, the fourth, pitching two innings in relief and giving up two runs in a game the Yankees won 6-2.

In 1957, he won 17 and lost nine with a 2.69 ERA and, in 1958, he had his first losing record in his Big League career, going 12-13 with a 4.17 ERA. From 1958 through 1966, nine years, he started 40 or more games every year.

In 1959, he was 17-13 and the Dodgers won the pennant again, this time beating the Chicago White Sox in six games. He started and won Game 3, 3-1, going seven innings and giving up just the one run.

In 1960, he was 15-14 and, in 1961, he was 13-10. 1962 was his best year in baseball, winning 25 and losing nine, with a 2.83 ERA. In 1963, he won 17 and lost 13 and the Dodgers went to the World Series again, sweeping the Yankees in four games. Drysdale pitched the finale, shutting out the Yankees, on three hits, for a complete game, 1-0 win.

He was a 6' 5", 190 pound, right handed, side arm pitcher who was intimidating and had no qualms about throwing at or close to batters to keep them off the plate. On his page at the Hall of Fame, he is quoted as saying that ' I hate hitters. I start a game mad and I stay that way until it's over. ' The great hitter Orlando Cepeda once said of him ' The trick against Drysdale is to hit him before he hits you. '

In 1964, he won 18 and lost 16 but, in 1965, came back to win 23 and lose 12 with a 2.77 ERA as the Dodgers won the pennant and beat the Minnesota Twins in seven games in the World Series. He got knocked out in the third inning and lost Game 1 of the Series, 8-2, but got the win in Game 4 as the Dodgers won 7-2. He had a .300 batting average that year, getting 39 hits in 130 at bats and hit seven homers for the second time in his career. He won the Cy Young Award and was named Major League Baseball's Player of the Year.

In 1966 he was only 13-16 as the Dodgers won the pennant but were swept by the Baltimore Orioles in the Series. Drysdale lost two games in the Series. In the first game, he was knocked out in the third inning as the Dodgers lost 5-2 and he pitched a complete game four hitter in Game 4 only to lose 1-0. In 1967 he was 13-16 again.

In 1968, he won 14 and lost 12 but had one of the most unbelievable streaks ever put together by a pitcher. It started on May 14, when he pitched a two hit, complete game shutout to beat the Chicago Cubs, 1-0. Four days later, he beat the Houston Astros, 1-0, pitching a complete game, five hit shutout. On May 22, he pitched another five hit, complete game shut out, this time beating the St. Louis Cardinals, 2-0.

On May 26, he went the route against Houston again, pitching a six hit shutout and winning 5-0. Five days later, he gave up six hits in another complete game shutout, beating the San Francisco Giants, 3-0. On June 4, he pitched a complete game, shutting out the Pittsburgh Pirates on three hits and winning 5-0.

In the space of 22 days he had pitched six complete game shutouts, giving up a total of 27 hits in 54 innings. In his next outing, on June 8, he held the Phillies scoreless for four innings before giving up a run on a sacrifice fly in the fifth inning, extending his scoreless string to 58 2/3 innings, an all time record that stood for 20 years until another Dodger, Orel Hershiser, put together a streak of 59 consecutive scoreless innings in 1988. Drysdale's 54 scoreless innings is still the second longest streak in baseball history.

1969 was his last year in baseball. At 33, he suffered a torn rotator cuff in his throwing arm and called it quits. That last year, before the injury, he was 5-4 in just 12 starts with a 4.45 ERA. He was named to the Hall of Fame in 1984.

He won 209 and lost 66 in his career, with a 2.95 ERA and 2,486 strikeouts. He pitched in eight All Star Games, led the league in strikeouts three times and in games started four times.

He was married to woman's basketball great, Ann Meyers, who was named to the Basketball Hall of Fame in 1993 and they were the only couple ever who were both named to the Hall of Fame in one of the four major sports.

Don Drysdale passed away, at the age of 56, on July 3, 1993, of a heart attack, just hours before he was scheduled to do the color commentary for the broadcast of game between the Montreal

Expos and the Dodgers. Ironically, his passing occurred less than one week after the death of Roy Campanella, his battery mate in his first two years with the Dodgers.

In 2012, Miguel Cabrera won the American League Triple Crown, symbolic of leading the league in batting average, home runs and runs batted in in the same year. He batted .330 with 44 homers and 139 RBI's. The last previous American League player to win the Crown was Carl Yastrzemski in 1967.

THE 1914 WORLD SERIES

In the 1914 World Series, played between the Boston Braves and the Philadelphia Athletics, the Braves swept the series in four games. The Braves, managed by George Stallings, had won the National League, an eight team league in those days, with a record of 94-59. The Athletics, owned and managed by Connie Mack, since 1901, had taken the American League, also an eight team league, with a 99-53 record. There were no playoffs in those days, the pennant winners in each league met in the World Series.

Both teams had exceptional starting pitching. The Braves had Dick Rudolph, 26-10 with 31 complete games and a 2.35 ERA in 336 innings pitched, Bill James, 26-7 with 30 complete games, a 1.90 ERA in 332 inning pitched and Lefty Tyler, 16-13 with 21 complete games, a 2.69 ERA and a mere 271 innings pitched.

The Athletics had more depth and balance with five starters, Bob Shawkey, 15-8, Bullet Joe Bush, 17-13, Eddie Plank, 15-7, Weldon Wyckoff, 11-7, and Chief Bender 17-3 with 69 complete games between them. The Athletics also had Herb Pennock, a 20 year old pitcher and future Hall of Famer who had won 11 and lost 4.

Going into the series, it looked to be a close match up with pitching the key and the Athletics looking like they had the edge with the depth in their pitching staff.

In Game 1, played on October 9, at the old Shibe Park in Philadelphia, before 20,562 fans, the Braves won 7-1 behind Dick Rudolph, who pitched a complete game, giving up just five hits and the one run, while Chief Bender took the loss, lasting just 5 1/3 innings and giving up six runs on eight hits before being relieved by Weldon Wyckoff who finished the game.

Catcher Hank Gowdy went 3 for 3 for the Braves, drove in one run, scored two others and had a double and triple. Center fielder 'Possum' Whitted and short stop 'Rabbit' Maranville each had two RBI's for the Braves in a game that lasted just one hour and fifty-eight minutes.

Game 2, was also at Shibe Park and 20,562 again turned out for the game. Bill James, who started and finished, on the mound for the Braves and the Phillies' Eddie Plank locked up in a pitcher's duel that had the game scoreless through the top of the ninth inning when Braves third baseman Charlie Deal doubled to center. He then stole third and right fielder Les Mann drove him in with a single to center for the win to put the Braves up two games to one. The game took one hour and 56 minutes to play.

The scene then shifted to Boston where the Braves home games were played in Fenway Park. On October 12, with 35,520 fans in attendance, Lefty Tyler started for the Braves and Bullet Joe Bush for the Athletics. The score was 2-2 after nine and both teams scored two in the tenth to make it 4-4, with Gowdy hitting the only homer of the series to start off the Braves half of the tenth. After ten innings, the Braves Bill James, who had just pitched a two hit shutout two days earlier came in to relieve Tyler and shut the Athletics down in the eleventh and twelfth innings.

In the bottom of the twelfth, Gowdy doubled to left for the Braves and pinch hitter Larry Gilbert was walked. When right fielder Herbie Moran tried a sacrifice bunt, Bush fielded it and threw wild to third allowing Gowdy to score the winning run. The Braves were up three games to none with the next game at home. The game took three hours and six minutes to play.

In Game 4, Dick Rudolph pitched his second complete game of the series, giving up just one run as the Braves won the game, 3-1, and completed the series sweep. 34,365 fans filled Fenway Park for the game which lasted just one hour and 49 minutes.

Bob Shawkey started for the A's and lasted just five innings before being relieved by Pennock who finished the game. Braves second baseman Johnny Evers, of Tinker to Evers to Chance fame, singled with the score tied at 1-1 in the last of the fifth to drive in the winning runs. Game 4 lasted just one hour and forty-nine minutes making the total playing time for the entire World Series eight hours and forty-nine minutes.

The Braves had swept the series using just three different pitchers in four games. Rudolph and James won two each and the only other pitcher to take the mound for the Braves was Tyler who lasted ten innings in Game 3. The Athletics had used just six different pitchers in the series for a total of nine pitchers in the four game series. By contrast, the Giants and Royals, in the 2014 series, used 11 different pitchers between them in the first two games.

One hundred years later in that 2014 World Series between the San Francisco Giants and the Kansas City Royals, there was another remarkable pitching performance turned in, this time by the Giants' young right hander, Madison Bumgarner. Not only did Bumgarner start and win Games 1 and 5, he came back in Game 7 on 2 days rest and pitched five scoreless innings to finish and win that game. There was no question he was the Most Valuable Player in the series.

In 1914 and 2014, pitching was the name of the game in the World Series. Over the last 100 years the development of specialists, in the form of short and long relievers, set up men, closers, and left handed specialists used mostly against left handed hitters, has changed the way pitchers are used but has not diminished the importance of pitching.

SECTION 21

On September 13, 1931, Rogers Hornsby, then with the Chicago Cubs, hit the first ever walk off, extra inning, pinch hit, grand slam home run in baseball history to beat the Boston Braves in eleven innings, 11-7.

THE 1964 WORLD SERIES

Fifty seasons after the 1914 World Series, on August 24, 1964, the Baltimore Orioles were in first place in the American League, two games ahead of the Chicago White Sox. The league was composed of ten teams, with no divisions that year as was the National League, where the Philadelphia Phillies led the league, 6 ½ games ahead of the San Francisco Giants.

In that year, the two league champions would play in the World Series with no playoff preceding it. Neither the League leading Orioles nor the Phillies would make it to the Big Show that year as the New York Yankees and St Louis Cardinals put together great streaks at the end of the season to win their respective league titles.

On August 24, the Yankees were in third place, five games behind the league leading Orioles and three games behind the second place Chicago White Sox. The Cardinals were in fourth place, ten full games behind the league leading Phillies, 3 ½ behind the second place Giants and three behind the third place Reds. The Cards won 27 and lost only 11 the rest of the way to end in first place at 93-69, one game ahead of the Phillies, while the Yankees were winning 28 and losing 11 to end at 99-63 and nose out the White Sox by one game.

The Yankees clinched the pennant on October 3, the next to last day of the season, beating the Cleveland Indians, 8-3 in Yankee Stadium. The game went to the last of the eighth tied 3-3.

Clete Boyer singled for the Yankees with one out and, after the second out, Phil Linz singled to left and Bobbie Richardson beat out a grounder to short to score Boyer. Roger Maris was walked to load the bases and Mickey Mantle walked to force in Linz with the second run. Elston Howard singled to center to score Richardson and Maris and Joe Pepitone drove in Mantle with a single to right and the Yankees were up 8-3.

Pedro Ramos came in in relief of Pete Mikkelson to pitch the ninth and shut the Indians down 1-2-3 and the Yankees had clinched the pennant with one game left. Mikkelson got the win and Ramos the save.

The Cards went to the last day of the National League season tied with the Cincinnati Reds for first place. The Cards were playing the Mets in the old Busch Stadium and pounded out 11 runs on 14 hits to win 11-5. Tim McCarver and Dick Groat had two doubles apiece for the Cards and Ken Boyer and Lou Brock also doubled. Bill White had a two run homer and Curt Flood also homered for the Cards. Curt Simmons started on the mound for the Cards but gave way to Bob Gibson, who pitched four innings in relief for the win.

While this was going on, the Philadelphia Phillies, behind a complete game, six hit shutout by Jim Bunning, who won his 19th game of the year, beat the Reds 10-0 to eliminate the Reds and move into a tie for second with them.

Between them, in an amazing six week period, the Yanks and Cards had put together a record of 55-22, a remarkable .714 winning percentage, at the end of the season, to make it to the World Series.

That year, the 'Say Hey Kid' Willy Mays led the National League with 47 homers while Hammerin' Harmon Killebrew led the American with 49. Ken Boyer won the National League MVP Award and Brooks Robinson the American, both third basemen, while Dean Chance won the Cy Young Award with a record of

20-9. There was only one Cy Young Award given until 1967 when the Award was changed to award one for each league.

In the World Series, the Cards won Game 1, at home, 9-5, with Ray Sadecki getting the win and Whitey Ford taking the loss, before just 30,805 fans in the old Busch Stadium. The Yankees came back and won Game 2, 8-3, behind Mel Stottlemeyer, who pitched a complete game, with St. Louis Ace Bob Gibson taking the loss.

Back in New York for Game 3, in front of a crowd of 67,101 in the old Yankee Stadium, the Yankees edged the Cards, 2-1, behind a complete game six hitter by Jim Bouton. Mickey Mantle hit a ninth inning, lead off, walk off home run, off reliever Barney Schultz to win the game for the Yankees.

The Cards came back in Game 4, to tie the series at two games apiece with a 4-3 victory. Ray Sadecki, who had won Game 1, gave up the Yankees three runs in the first before getting the second out but Roger Craig, who came in with one out in the first, got the win in relief, and Ron Taylor, who got the save, shut the Yankees out the rest of the way as the Cards bested Yankee hurler Al Downing.

Game 5 went to ten innings before St. Louis catcher Tim McCarver, hit a three run homer to give the Cards a 5-2 win and take them back to St Louis leading the series three games to two. The Cardinals' Bob Gibson pitched a complete ten inning game, giving up just six hits, for the win, while Yankee reliever Pete Mikkelsen who gave up McCarver's homer, took the loss.

The teams returned to St Louis where the Yankees extended the series to seven games by taking Game 6, 8-3. Jim Bouton got his second win of the series for the Yankees as they scored five in the eighth highlighted by a grand slam homer by Yankee first baseman Joe Pepitone. Pepitone's homer, like Mantle's that won Game 3, was hit by the first batter faced by a reliever, in this case, Gordie Richardson.

In Game 7, the Cards behind Bob Gibson again, won 7-5, to take the series four games to three. Gibson went the distance for the win, although he gave up nine hits, including homers by Boyer, Linz and Mantle. Stottlemeyer started for New York but was lifted after giving up three runs in the fourth and Al Downing, his relief, immediately gave up a homer to the first batter he faced, Lou Brock, and the Cards got three in the fifth to take the lead. The Yanks came back to score two in the ninth on Linz's and Boyer's homers but it was too little too late and the Cards had won the World Series.

Bob Gibson was named the Most Valuable Player, an honor he would earn again in 1967. He also won the Cy Young Award in 1968 and 1970 and was National League MVP in 1968. He averaged an amazing 17 complete games a year in his 17 year career with the Cardinals.

Clete Boyer played third base for the Yankees in the series and his brother, Ken, played third for the Cardinals and each player started every game at that position for his team. Both brothers had homers in Game 7.

Future Hall of Fame members Lou Brock and Bob Gibson played for the Cardinals and Whitey Ford and Mickey Mantle played for the Yankees and Yogi Berra managed the team. Cardinal Catcher Tim McCarver later earned the Ford Frick Award from the HOF for his contributions to the game as a broadcaster.

The finish of the 1964 season and the World Series that followed was one of baseball's most exciting finishes ever.

SECTION 22

Cy Young, who pitched from 1890 until 1911, won the most games in Major League history, with 511, while losing 316, also the most in history. The right hander started a total of 815 games in his 22 year career and completed an unbelievable 749 of them. Both the number of starts and the number of complete games are also all time records.

DAVID WELLS

On the 17th of May, 1998, David 'Boomer' Wells pitched the thirteenth perfect game in baseball history since 1900. He did it in Yankee Stadium, before 49,820 fans and he did it in just 2 hours and 40 minutes. The win brought his record for the year to 5-1 but, at the time, he had an earned run average of 4.45.

He struck out 11 batters while facing the minimum of 27 over nine innings as the Yankees beat the Minnesota Twins 4-0. The win brought the Yankees record to 28 wins and 9 losses and left them 3 ½ games in first place in the American League East. He struck out the side in the third inning and got two strikeouts in each of the fifth and sixth innings.

The Yankees had taken over the lead in the Eastern Division on April 30 and would remain in first place the rest of the season. They won 114 and lost just 48 to finish 22 games ahead of the second place Boston Red Sox that year.

The Yankees, facing LaTroy Hawkins, who would later pitch for them, managed only six hits in the game. Offensively, it was the Bernie Williams Show for the Yankees as their center fielder doubled in the second inning, went to third on a passed ball and scored on a wild pitch to put them ahead 1-0.

In the fourth, with two outs, Williams hit the first pitch he saw for a homer to make it 2-0 and, in the seventh, he doubled and scored the Yankees third run when designated hitter Darryl Strawberry tripled to drive him in. Left fielder Chad Curtis singled to score Strawberry with the only other run of the game.

Remarkably, in his last start prior to the perfect game, on May 12, Wells had retired the last ten batters he faced, making it 37 batters in a row he had faced without allowing a base runner. The perfect game was the first by a Yankee pitcher since Don Larsen's perfect game in the 1956 World Series. The perfect game occurred three days before his 35th birthday. He was born in Torrance, California on May 20, 1963.

In the American League Division Series that year, the Yankees faced the Texas Rangers and swept them in three games. In Game 1, Wells started and pitched eight shut out innings as the Yankees won 2-0. With Andy Pettitte and David Cone starting the next two games, the Yankees would hold the Rangers to just one run and 13 hits in the three games.

In the American League Championship Series he won two games, pitching 15 2/3 innings, striking out 18 and giving up just 5 runs against the Cleveland Indians asthe Yankees won in five games. He won Games 1 and 5 and was named Most Valuable Player in the series.

The Yankees went on to sweep the San Diego Padres in the World Series and Wells started and won Game 1. The World Series win was the first of three consecutive Series wins for the Yankees and came in their first year under new General Manager Brian Cashman. It was Manager Joe Torre's second World Championship in three years with the Yankees.

The Boomer, as Wells was called, was drafted by the Toronto Blue Jays in the 1982 draft and made his major league debut for them, against the Yankees, on June 30, 1987 and gave up nine hits and four runs in four innings getting the loss.

He played for nine different Major League teams in his 21 year career, the Blue Jays, Yankees, Detroit Tigers, San Diego Padres, Boston Red Sox, Cincinnati Reds, Baltimore Orioles, Chicago White Sox and Los Angeles Dodgers, some of them more than once, from 1987 until 2007. He played for six different teams in post season play, including four of the five from the American League Eastern Division, the Yankees, Red Sox, Orioles and Blue Jays. He also played in the post season with the National League Padres and Reds.

He appeared in 27 post season games, winning 10 and losing 5, with a 3.17 ERA, including 7 World Series games where he was 1-1 and had an ERA of 3.72.

He made his last appearance at age 44, on September 28, 2007, as a member of the Los Angeles Dodgers, lasting six innings, giving up just two earned runs on seven hits, and getting the win against the San Francisco Giants.

He was in three World Series, two with the Yankees and one with the Blue Jays and was named to three All Star teams. In 1999 and 2000, he led American League pitchers in complete games with seven and nine.

Wells finished the 1998 season with a record of 18-4 and a 3.49 ERA in 214 innings pitched. The previous year, with the Yankees, he had won 16 and lost 10.

On February 18, 1999, the Yankees traded Wells, Homer Bush and Graeme Lloyd to the Toronto Blue Jays for another pretty good pitcher, Roger Clemens.

In the next two years with the Jays, Wells was 17-10 and 20-8, the only time he won 20 games in his career and his 20 was the highest win total in the league in 2000. In the four year period from 1997-2000, he won 71 and lost 32 with the Yankees and Blue Jays. In his career, he won 239 and lost just 157, winning ten or more games in 14 different seasons.

David Wells had a long career in baseball but never had a greater moment than when Minnesota shortstop and number nine hitter Pat Meares flied out to Paul O'Neill in right for the last out of the perfect game in the old Yankee Stadium.

SECTION 23

Nolan Ryan recorded the most strikeouts in a single season, by a pitcher, since 1900, with 383 in 1973. Sandy Koufax has the second highest total in that period with 382 in 1965 and Randy Johnson the third highest with 372 in 2001.

THE 2004 RED SOX COMEBACK

In 2004, the Yankees won the American League East with a record of 101-61 and the Red Sox finished in second place in the East, thee games back with a 98-64 record. By virtue of having the best record of the second place teams, the Sox made the Wild Card and played the Western Division Champion Anaheim Angels.

The Sox, behind Curt Schilling, easily took Game 1 of the Division Series at Anaheim, 9-3, with a two run homer by Kevin Millar and a three run homer by Manny Ramirez in the fourth being the big hits. In Game 2, after Pedro Martinez had held the Angels to three runs on six hits for seven innings, the Sox led 4-3 going to the ninth. They then got four in the top of the with the big hit a three run, bases clearing double by shortstop Orlando Cabrera to win 8-3 and go up two games to one going back to Boston for Game 3.

In Game 3, the Sox were up 6-1 going to the seventh behind Bronson Arroyo, who left ahead 6-1 after walking the lead off hitter in the seventh. Mike Myers replaced him and walked Jamie Molina and Mike Timlin replaced Myers. After getting two outs and loading the bases Timlin walked in a run and then gave up a grand slam to Vladimir Gurrero to tie the game at 6-6.

The game went to the tenth inning still tied and Johnny Damon singled to center to lead off the inning. With two out, David Ortiz hit a walk off homer and the Sox had won the Division Series and would play the Yankees in the League Championship

Series.

The Yankees had gotten by the Central Division winning Twins in the ALDS, three games to one. New York won the first two games at home by scores of 10-7 and 3-1 and then got 22 hits to win 19-8 in Game 3, in Fenway, and no one could have believed that the Red Sox were not done for the season.

No team, in any of the major sports, had ever come from behind three games to none to win a playoff series and things did not look good for the Sox.

In Game 4, it looked like it was all over for the Sox as they trailed 2-0 going to the last of the fifth but they got three to go ahead 3-2. The Yankees came back with two in the top of the sixth to go up 4-3 and it went to the last of the ninth that way.

With the Great Mariano Rivera in to close for the Yankees, it seemed like the Red Sox season was over. Then, third baseman Bill Mueller singled to drive in the tying run in the person of Dave Roberts, who had stolen second base when put in to run for first baseman Kevin Millar, and the game went into extra innings.

In the last of the twelfth, with reliever Paul Quantrill on the mound for the Yankees, left fielder Manny Ramirez got a lead off single and the next batter, DH David Ortiz, hit a home run to win the game 6-4. The Sox were still alive, barely.

Trailing 4-2 and appearing to be finished again in the eighth inning of Game 5, the Sox scored twice on a homer by Ortiz and a sacrifice fly by Trot Nixon to tie the game at 4-4.

It stayed that way until the last of the fourteenth when, with Rivera pitching again, Damon singled, Ramirez walked and Ortiz drove in Damon with a single to give the Red Sox their second consecutive come from behind extra inning win against the best closer in baseball history in another elimination game.

However, the Sox still trailed three games to two and were facing another elimination game as the Series went back to New York.

The Sox won Game six, scoring four in the fourth, the big hit a three run homer by Mark Bellhorn, to win 4-2 behind a great pitching performance by Curt Schilling. Schilling went seven innings, giving up just one run on four hits and, after Bronson Arroyo gave up a run in the eighth to make it 4-2, Keith Foulke pitched a scoreless ninth despite giving up two walks, for the save.

Game 7 was almost anticlimactic as the Sox got a two run homer from Ortiz in the first, a grand slam from Damon in the second and another two run homer from Damon in the fourth to lead 8-1 after four innings and go on to win easily by a score of 10-3. The Sox had done the impossible and would go on to the World Series.

David Ortiz, who had 12 hits in 31 at bats in the series, with three home runs and 11 RBI's, was named the series Most Valuable Player. In the 10 post season games, Ortiz had gone 18 for 42, a .429 batting average.

The Sox would go on to sweep the St. Louis Cardinals, winners of the National League pennant, in the World Series in four games. The Cardinals had won 105 and lost 57, a win total surpassed in the previous twenty years only by the 1998 Yankees, with 114 wins, and the 1986 New York Mets with 108. Yet, the Sox handled them with ease, winning by scores of 11-9, 6-2, 4-1 and 3-0, outscoring them 24-12 for the series and holding them to three runs in the last three games.

Keith Foulke got the win in relief for the Sox in Game 1 and also got the save in Game 4. Curt Schilling, Pedro Martinez and Derek Lowe started Games 2, 3 and 4 and all three got the wins. Sox left fielder, Manny Ramirez, who got seven hits in seventeen at bats including a homer in Game 4, was named Most Valuable

Player in the Series. Center fielder Johnny Damon also had six hits in 21 at bats including two doubles, a triple, home run, two RBI's and scored four runs.

As sweet as it was for Red Sox fans to have their first World's Championship in eighty-six years, the win over the Yankees in the League Championship Series, coming from so far down, was almost as good.

The final game in the 2004 series was on the road for the Sox and when they won again in 2007, the final game was on the road again, so it wasn't until 2013 that they would clinch a World Series at home in Fenway. In 2013, they defeated the St. Louis Cardinals, 6-1, in Game 6, to take the series 4 games to 2 to clinch the World Series in front of the Fenway faithful for the first time since 1918, 95 years before.

There have been only fifteen Triple Crown Winners in baseball since 1900. Only the St. Louis Cardinals' Rogers Hornsby, who won the Triple Crown in 1922 and 1925, and Ted Williams, of the Boston Red Sox, who won in 1942 and 1947, have won it more than once.

ORIOLE PARK AT CAMDEN YARD

There are many new, modern and fan friendly ball parks that have been constructed throughout Major League Baseball over the past twenty years. Safeco Field in Seattle, home of the Seattle Mariners, which replaced the old, drab, King Dome, has the advantage of a retractable roof as does Chase Field in Phoenix, home of the Arizona Diamondbacks, and others, allowing play no matter the weather. Some of the other new ball parks, including the new Yankee Stadium and Citi Field in New York, home of the Mets, lack the roof but have many of the same fan friendly amenities.

For my money, the best of the newer ball parks, from a fan's perspective, is Oriole Park at Camden Yard which was completed in 1992. It was built with public funds generated from the Maryland Lottery at a cost of only 110 million dollars.

The location was the site of the old Baltimore and Ohio Railroad Yards which contained the longest building on the east coast, a warehouse 1,016 feet long. The original plan for the ball park called for the warehouse to be torn down but the final plan kept the warehouse and incorporated it into the ballpark. The entire rest of the railroad yard was torn up to make room for the ballpark.

By keeping the warehouse and making that part of Eutaw Street that runs between it and the stadium proper into a pedestrian walkway, and placing gates at each end controlling access, the planners greatly enhanced the attraction of the ballpark.

The Red Sox have done a similar thing with making Yawkey Way almost a part of the ball park but the area lacks the inviting atmosphere of Eutaw street. The warehouse building provides a backdrop for center field around to beyond the right field foul line and its presence is felt everywhere within the stadium.

Fans entering the complex through Gate H, which allows them into Eutaw Street and opens one hour prior to the gates to the stadium proper, find themselves walking past a statue of Babe Ruth into an area bounded on one side by the warehouse and the other by the ballpark. All along both sides of the street, which runs from roughly behind center field, are shops and restaurants, including Boog Powell's Barbecue Stand and even a viewing area where early fans can watch batting practice from outside the stadium.

In addition to the first floor attractions in the warehouse, there is a catwalk connecting the fourth floor where the club's offices are located with the club level in the stadium. Club level seating is luxurious, available to the general public and costs just slightly more than regular seating.

Pregame time on Eutaw Street is as much a part of any visit to Camden Yard as the ball game itself. Fans from all over the east coast can be found on any given day and, when the Yankees or Red Sox are in town, you can bet there will be as many or more visiting team jerseys in the crowd as home jerseys.

On Eutaw Street, there are baseball shaped plaques that commemorate the landing location of any ball hit onto the street from the ball park on the fly with information identifying the date and the player who hit the ball. Only one ball has ever been struck which hit the warehouse on the fly and that was hit by Ken Griffey, Jr. in the home run derby at the 1993 All Star Game.

Throughout the street there are picnic tables and rest room facilities for the convenience of fans. An outdoor roof deck has been added in center-field with a full service bar and comfortable seating accessed by any ticketed fan. There are statues of Oriole legends Eddie Murray, Jim Palmer, Cal Ripken, Brooks Robinson, Frank Robinson and Earl Weaver located along the pedestrian walkway.

Another big attraction of Camden Yard is its proximity to the trendy Inner Harbor area of Baltimore. In addition to being able to shop the fashionable indoor/outdoor Inner Harbor shopping area, visit the Baltimore Aquarium, Fort McHenry or Little Italy and enjoy music and other entertainment throughout the harbor area, fans can walk from there out Pratt Street to the ball game comfortably and safely.

Within a short walk of the ballpark is the Babe Ruth Birthplace and Museum housed in what was once the Babe's home. The museum has many interesting exhibits and memorabilia from the Babe and his era. Until recently, the Sports Legends Museum was also located adjacent to the ball park but a problem with the leasing of the building has forced the Museum, which contained exhibits of football, basketball and other sports as well as railroad and other exhibits to look for a new home.

The route from the Babe Ruth Museum to and from the ballpark is marked with 60 baseballs in the sidewalk, memorializing Babe's long standing record output of sixty homers in one season set in 1927.

The ball park itself holds 48,876 fans. There are no bad seats and prices are generally cheaper than in most parks in the northeast. Its location allows for easy access to and from Rte. 95 and there is garage and lot parking throughout the area minimizing the congestion before and after games.

Baltimore did as Seattle did, building the football and baseball stadiums in close proximity to each other which allows crowds from each to use the same parking and other facilities. M & T Bank Stadium, the home of the Baltimore Ravens of the National Football League, was completed in 1998 and seats 71,008 fans.

Camden Yard has the charm of an old style ballpark with all the amenities of the newer ballparks and, for my money provides the best environment in which to watch a baseball game. The only drawback to this ballpark is the lack of a roof which can make for uncomfortable conditions in the early or late season.

Pete Rose played more games in his career than anyone else in baseball history, with 3,562. Carl Yastzremski, with 3,308, had the next highest and Hank Aaron, with 3,298, is third. Iron Man Cal Ripken, who holds the record for most consecutive games played had 3,001 for the fourth highest total.

THE LONGEST MAJOR LEAGUE GAMES

The longest game, from the perspective of time, ever played in Major League baseball history started on May 8, 1984 and ended on May 9, 1984. The game lasted eight hours and six minutes. At the end of 17 innings, with the score tied at 3-3, the game was suspended and resumed the following day.

The game was played at Comiskey Park in Chicago, between the Chicago White Sox, who would finish in sixth place in the seven team Western Division of the American League, and the Milwaukee Brewers, who would finish in last place in the Eastern Division. A crowd of just 14,754 were on hand for the game. Tony LaRussa, who would later be named to the Hall of Fame as a Manager, was in his sixth year with the White Sox and Rene Lachemann was the Brewers Manager.

The game was resumed on May 9, before the regularly scheduled game between the two teams. The score remained tied, 3-3, through the 20th inning. In the top of the 21st inning, with Ron Reed, Chicago's sixth pitcher on the mound, and two outs, Milwaukee designated hitter, Cecil Cooper, beat out an infield single to second base and first baseman Ted Simmons walked. Left fielder Ben Ogilvie than homered to make it 6-3 going to the last of the 21st and it looked like it was going to end there.

In the bottom of the 21st, with Milwaukee's sixth and last pitcher, Chuck Porter, on the mound, Chicago center fielder Rudy Law got to second on an error by third baseman Randy Ready. Chicago Catcher Carlton Fisk singled to drive in Law and first baseman Marc Hill singled to left. Harold Baines was walked to load the bases and left fielder Tom Paciorek singed up the middle to score Fisk and Law with the tying runs and the game went to the 22nd.

After Porter got the first batter to strike out in the 25th inning, Harold Baines hit the 753rd pitch of the game for a walk off homer and the White Sox had won the game 7-6. Chicago had sent 104 batters to the plate in the game and Milwaukee 94.

Tom Seaver, who came in in relief and pitched a scoreless top of the 25th for Chicago got the win and then went out and started the regularly scheduled game, went 8 1/3 innings there, and got his second win of the day as the Sox won 5-4.

In the regular game, Seaver gave up just three hits, but a three run homer by first baseman Roy Howell, in the seventh, and a solo homer by short stop Robin Yount in the ninth accounted for all the Brewers scoring. Seaver ended his Hall of Fame career with 311 wins and 205 losses and a career ERA of 2.86.

Carlton Fisk caught the entire 26 innings of the first game for the White Sox and came in to pinch run in the seventh inning of the regularly scheduled game and caught the last two innings. Fisk, who played 24 years, from 1969 to 1980 with the Red Sox, before signing with the White Sox as a Free Agent in 1981 and playing with the White Sox until 1993, was also elected to the Hall of Fame.

The longest game, measured by innings, in Major League baseball history, took place on May 1, 1920 between the Brooklyn Robins, who later became the Brooklyn and then Los Angeles Dodgers, and the Boston Braves. The game, ended in a tie when it was called after 26 innings and counted as a tie in the standings.

The Robins, managed by Wilbert Robinson, who was later inducted in the Hall of Fame, as a Manager, got a run to go up 1-0 in the fifth inning when second baseman Ivy Olson drove in catcher Ernie Kruger. The Braves, managed by George Stallings, tied it at 1-1 in the sixth as third baseman Tony Boeckel drove in right fielder Walter Cruise with the tying run.

A crowd of approximately 4,500 watched as the 26 inning game was played in just three hours and fifty minutes. The Robins sent 90 players to the plate in the game and the Braves 96. There were 24 hits in the game, resulting in just the two runs, fifteen by the Braves and nine by the Dodgers. Joe Oeschger started on the mound for the Braves and Leon Cadore for the Robins. Unbelievably, they both pitched the entire 26 innings and were still on the mound when the game was called because of darkness. Cadore struck out seven and walked five and Oeschger struck out seven and walked four.

Cadore had a 10 year career and won just 68 games and lost 72, mostly with Brooklyn. After his playing career he married Mae Tebbets, whose father, Charlie Ebbets, owned the Brooklyn franchise, hence the name of their ball park, Ebbets Field. Ebbets Field was completed in 1913 in the Flatbush section of Brooklyn and opened with an exhibition game against the New York Yankees on April 5, 1913.

Oeschger pitched for twelve years, winning 82 and losing 116. He was with the Phillies, Giants and Braves before ending his career with Brooklyn. In 1920 and 1921, with the Braves, he had his most productive years, winning 35 and losing 27 including 20 wins in 1920.

After the 26 inning game, the Robins traveled back to Brooklyn, where they played the Phillies at Ebbets Field on the next day. That game went 13 innings before the Phillies won 4-3. George Smith went the entire 13 innings for the Phillies and got the win while Burleigh Grimes went the complete game for the Robins and got the loss. Grimes, who had a 19 year career, winning 270 and losing 212 was later elected to the Hall of Fame.

The next day, the Robins were back in Boston where they played a nineteen inning game before losing to the Braves 2-1. They got another complete game out of Sherry Smith who went 18 1/3 before giving up the winning run in the last of the 19th. Dana Fillingham pitched the entire 19 innings for the Braves for the win giving up just one run on 12 hits.

The Robins had played 58 innings in three games in three days and had two losses and a tie to show for it but had used just three pitchers. If this is not strange enough, the loss to the Phillies was the first of seven consecutive one run games the Robins would play, five of which they lost.

At the end of that stretch, the Robins were in fourth place. They would go on to win the National League pennant with a record of 93 wins and 61 losses and lose the World Series to the Cleveland Indians five games to two.

SECTION 26

Since 1900, only 14 players have hit four home runs in a single game. Lou Gehrig, of the Yankees, was the first American Leaguer, on June 3, 1932, while Chuck Klein of the Phillies, was first in the National League on July 10, 1936. Josh Hamilton, of the Texas Rangers, on May 8, 2012, was the latest to do so in the American League and Shawn Green, of the Los Angeles Dodgers, the latest in the National League on May 23, 2002.

DON ZIMMER

On July 2, 1954, the Brooklyn Dodgers beat the Philadelphia Phillies, 7-6, in Connie Mack Stadium in Philadelphia. The Phillies scored three runs in the last of the eighth to take the lead, 7-5, and held on to win when the Dodgers scored once in the top of the ninth.

The Dodger lineup that day included such all time Dodger greats as Junior Gilliam in right field, Jackie Robinson in left field, Gil Hodges at first base, Roy Campanella catching and Carl Furillo in center field. Future Hall of Famers Outfielder Duke Snyder and Shortstop Pee Wee Reese were in the dugout but not playing that day.

Twenty-three year old Donald William Zimmer, who passed away in 2014, made his major league debut in that game, replacing Reese at shortstop. At 5'9", 165 pounds, he was small even by that day's standards. Zimmer got a triple his first time up, going one for two with a walk and scoring twice in the defeat. He batted eighth in the lineup and got his triple in the third inning off Curt Simmons, one of the aces of the Phillies staff. He had been 17-8 in 1950 when, with Hall of Famer Robin Roberts winning 20 and losing 11, they had powered the Phillies into the World Series before being swept by the Yankees in four games.

Zimmer had been drafted in the Amateur draft in 1949 by the Dodgers and had played in the minors before making his debut. He had hit .310 at Mobile in the AA Southern Association in 1952 and .300 and .291 at St. Paul in the AAA American Association in 1953 and 1954.

In July of 1953, he was hit in the head with a pitch and almost died and was not expected to be able to come back to baseball. His injury led to the adoption of batting helmets in the major leagues and, according to Wickipedia, Yankee great Phil Rizzuto was the first player to wear a helmet.

Zim overcame his injury and played with the Dodgers from 1954 until 1959, moving from Brooklyn to Los Angeles with the team in 1958. He had a mediocre career at the plate with the Dodgers, while playing second, third and short, with a .228 batting average and just 43 homers and 161 RBIs.

In 1955, playing in just 88 games, he hit 15 homers and helped the Dodgers to the World Series championship. In 1960, he was traded to the Chicago Cubs and, in 1961, he was claimed by the new New York Mets in the expansion draft.

After going hit less in his first 34 at bats with the Mets in 1962, he was traded to the Cincinnati Reds. In 1963, he was traded back to the Dodgers and later that same season purchased from the Dodgers by the Washington Senators. He was with Washington until they released him in November of 1965 and his major league playing career ended.

In 12 years in the Major Leagues, he played in 1,095 games and had a career batting average of .235. He was a member of the Brooklyn Dodger team that beat the Yankees in the World Series in 1955 and the Los Angeles Dodger team that beat the Chicago White Sox in the World Series in 1959.

He played and coached in the Minor leagues for the next few

years and, from 1972 until shortly before his death in 2014, he was a coach, manager or served a major league team in some other capacity. He coached with the San Diego Padres, Boston Red Sox, New York Yankees, Chicago Cubs, San Francisco Giants, Colorado Rockies and Tampa Bay Rays.

He managed the San Diego Padres, Boston Red Sox, Texas Rangers and Chicago Cubs. In twelve seasons as a Manager, his teams won 885 games and lost 858. His Red Sox years were his most productive as a Manager, winning 411 and losing just 304 for a .575 won/loss percentage. With the Cubs, in 1989, he was named National League Manager of the year, when he led the Cubs to a 93-69 season, as they won the National League East and were defeated in the NLCS by the San Francisco Giants.

In perhaps his most visible position, he was Yankee Manager Joe Torre's Bench Coach from 1996 through 2003, the Yankees Glory Years, when they were in six World Series and won four of them. From 2004 until 2014, he served as Bench Coach and Special Advisor to the Tampa Bay Rays.

He spent 66 years in baseball and, upon joining the Rays, began to wear a uniform number that conformed to the number of years he had spent in baseball, wearing number 66 at the start of the 2014 season.

With his short stature and muscular build, he acquired the nickname Popeye and was something of a character. No one ever disputed Zim's baseball sense which was revered throughout the baseball world. He was a great store of baseball knowledge and lore and renowned as a story teller.

He coauthored two books and I would recommend the entertaining and informative book 'Zim: A Baseball Life' to anyone interested in the history of baseball.

Zimmer was proud to say that he never received a pay check in his life that did not come from baseball and he was a fierce competitor. In the 2003 American League Championship Series between the Yankees and Red Sox, at age 72, during a bases clearing brawl, Zim charged Red Sox pitcher Pedro Martinez and ended up being thrown to the ground.

He had a great sense of humor. While he was with the Yankees, Zim was hit with a foul ball by Chuck Knoblach and came to the ballpark the next day with an army helmet with the Yankee logo on it. Over the last few years of his career, one of my favorite sights in baseball was to look into the Rays dugout in Tropicana Field and see Zim sitting there looking like the 'Baseball Gnome ' with his round body and red cheeks.

He married his high school sweetheart, Jean, in 1951 at home plate before an Elmira, New York, minor league game and they were married 62 years. Looking back, no one could have expected anything else from the man who spent his entire adult life in the game. Baseball has been a different and less entertaining place without Don Zimmer.

Rickey Henderson holds the all time career record for stolen bases with 1,406 thefts, while Lou Brock, with 938, is a distant second. Both are Hall of Fame Members and Henderson holds the single season record, for players since 1900, with 130 steals while Brock had the second highest total with 118.

THE WILLIAMS SHIFT

In July of 1946, as the story goes, in an attempt to cool off Red Sox slugger Ted Williams, Lou Boudreau, then Manager of the Cleveland Indians, devised an infield shift between games of a double header.

In the first game of the doubleheader that day, the Red Sox had beaten the Indians 11-10 and Williams, who at that time was called Terrific Ted, had gone 4 for 5 with 3 home runs and a single and had driven in 8 runs. In his first time up in the nightcap, (for those of you who have never seen a single admission doubleheader, that's what the second game was called), Williams hit a double down the right field line.

The next time Ted came to the plate, in the third inning, Boudreau positioned his fielders in what became known as the Williams shift. The shift positioned third baseman Kenny Keltner behind second base, with no one between him and third base; Boudreau, who, as well as managing, played shortstop, moved to the right, or first base side, of second base, almost to the normal second base position; the second baseman, Jack Conway, moved back onto the outfield grass and closer to first base and the first baseman, Jimmy Wasdell, played on the foul line behind first base.

The center fielder, Pat Seerey, moved over into the normal right fielder's position and the right fielder, Hank Edwards, took a position on the right field foul line. The left fielder, George Case, moved in behind the normal shortstop position about 30 feet behind the infield.

Ted tried to hit through the shift and hit a ground ball which Boudreau, playing the normal second base position, fielded and threw him out. In his next two at bats Ted was walked so the shift wasn't tested.

In the World Series between the Red Sox and St. Louis Cardinals that year, the Cardinals used that shift to combat Williams' hitting. In that series, Ted got just five hits in 25 at bats after hitting .342 with a .667 slugging percentage, 38 homers and 123 RBI's during the regular season.

He struck out five times during the series, drove in just one run and scored two as the Sox lost to the Cardinals four games to three. In Game 3, which the Sox won, 4-0, he did bunt to third for a single to beat the shift.

Although the Williams shift has generally been believed to have been the first of its kind, it appears that the first shift of this kind was used in the twenties against a hitter, coincidentally named Cy Williams, no relation to Ted.

Cy was a left handed hitting outfielder who played for the Chicago Cubs and Philadelphia Phillies from 1912 – 1930. He had a career batting average of .292 and hit 251 homers. Manager Bill McKechnie, of the Reds, called Cy the ' most consistent right field hitters that ever lived ' and National League teams used what McKechnie called the Williams shift against him in the twenties.

Tom Swope, the Sports Editor of the Cincinnati Post at the time, wondered why, when faced with the shift, Cy didn't bunt toward third. Many of us are still asking that question when we see a radical shift today.

Baseball rules require that all players, with the exception of the catcher, be stationed within the foul lines of the field. The catcher's box is behind home plate, outside the foul lines but the area in which the catcher must be when the ball is released is outlined by lines on the field behind the batter's box.

The only other restriction on the location of a player is that the pitcher must deliver the pitch with one foot in contact with the pitching rubber atop the mound. The other players' positions are dictated by tradition only and are arbitrary so long as they remain within the foul lines.

Defensive players have always been moved around to defend against the abilities and tendencies of the batter and the pitcher and to be better able to react in certain situations. This has been true since long before Boudreau came up with his shift but the radical shifts are relatively new. Because of the need to keep the first baseman near the bag, to be able to get to the bag with the ball before the runner, radical shifts were generally only used against left handed hitters, although they have become more common against right handers in recent years.

In today's Major Leagues, in this age of computers, more and more information about the opposition is available to managers and coaches. Every at bat, including every pitch, is recorded and that record is available to all teams. Therefore, if a batter hits 80 or 90 percent of the pitches he puts in play in a certain location, the opposition has access to that information and has the ability to adjust its defense radically to defend that batter.

Some managers and teams pay more attention to this information than others. In the case of the Tampa Bay Rays, when Manager Joe Maddon was managing there, they employed different shifts, similar to the Williams shift, probably more than any other team in baseball. There are different opinions as to the effectiveness of such shifts and little evidence for or against their use.

One study reported by John Dewan, of ACTA Sports, after the

2011 season, which tracked the effect of the shift on several players during 2010 and 2011 showed significant decreases in batting averages for some specific players such as David Ortiz, Ryan Howard, Carlos Pena, Adam Dunn and Prince Fielder when the shift was employed against them.

Over the past several years, almost every version of the shift has been tried, including Maddon's Rays playing with five infielders and only two outfielders when the winning run was on third with no outs in the 2008 World Series.

It's puzzling to me why more left handed batters do not bunt to the left side against the shift as Williams did in the 1946 World Series. In Spring Training of 2013, I watched John Farrell's Red Sox put the shift on against Baltimore's Matt Wieters and Chris Davis, two left handed power hitters hitting back to back with no outs. Both batters dropped bunts down the third base side for easy hits and the Orioles had two men on and no out. It would seem that attacking the shift in this manner more often would discourage its use.

Bunting, however, has become a lost art as fewer and fewer teams use the bunt to sacrifice runners into scoring position. The book and movie Money Ball postulated that the bunt was the waste of an out and most teams, instead of sacrificing a runner, try to hit the ball to the right side in a sacrifice situation rather than giving up the out by bunting.

Charles Dillon 'Casey' Stengel managed the New York Yankees from 1949 until 1960. In that 12 year period, the team won the American League Pennant 10 times and the World Series seven times, including five consecutive World Series victories, from 1949 until 1953, the longest such streak in Major League history.

1963 WORLD SERIES

In 1963, the Major Leagues consisted of 10 teams. There was no wild card and no divisions in either of the leagues, the ten teams in each league played the full season of 162 games and the two winners met in the World Series. The names of most of the teams were the same as they are today, with the exception of the Houston franchise which was then called the Colt 45's and played in the National League.

The previous two seasons, 1961 and 1962, the New York Yankees had won the World Series over Fred Hutchinson's Cincinnati Reds, in 1961, four games to one, and over Alvin Dark's San Francisco Giants, in 1962, in seven games.

The 1961 Yankees had been powered by Roger Maris and Mickey Mantle with a total of 115 homers between them. Of course, Maris' 61 homers beat the previous record of 60 held by Babe Ruth but earned an asterisk in the record books because it was done over a 162 game season instead of the 154 games in which the Babe accomplished his.

Going into the 1963 season, the Yankees had seemed to be the team to beat in the American League. They had plenty of pitching led by Whitey Ford, Al Downing and Jim Bouton and their roster included five players whose numbers would eventually be retired by the Yankees, Mantle, Maris, Ford, Yogi

Berra and Elston Howard. Berra, Mantle and Maris were aging and nearing the ends of their Yankee careers but people like Howard, Joe Pepitone, Tom Tresh, Tony Kubek, Bobby Richardson and Clete Boyer still made for a formidable lineup.

The Los Angeles Dodgers, had a great pitching staff with Sandy Koufax, Don Drysdale and Johnny Podres leading the rotation and Maury Wills, Tommy Davis, John Roseboro, Jim Gilliam and Frank Howard gave them a strong offense.

The Yankees won the American League with a record of 104 wins and 57 losses to beat out the second place Chicago White Sox by 10 ½ games while the Washington Senators finished in last place with 106 losses, 48 ½ games back. The Red Sox won 76 and lost 85 to finish in seventh place.

Ford won 24 and lost only seven games while Elston Howard, who hit .287, with 28 homers and 85 RBIs, won the Most Valuable Player Award, the first ever won by an African American player.

The Dodgers won the National League almost as easily with 99 wins and 63 losses to beat the second place St. Louis Cardinals by 6 games. The New York Mets were in last place with a sad 111 losses, 48 games back and those Houston Colt 45's finished next to last with 96 losses.

Dodger left fielder, Tommy Davis, won the batting title with an average of .326 after winning it the previous year with a .346 average, 230 hits and 153 RBI's. Koufax won 25 and lost only 5, struck out 306 batters in 311 innings and won the Cy Young and Most Valuable Player awards.

Until 1967, only one Cy Young award was made annually to the best pitcher in all of baseball. Drysdale won 19 games, and had 17 complete games in 42 starts, the second of four years where he exceeded forty starts per year. Podres won 14 and lost 12 and had five complete game shutouts.

The Yankees and Dodgers opened up what was expected to be a close series on October 2 at Yankee Stadium before 69,000 fans. The great Sandy Koufax started on the mound for the Dodgers and struck out the first five Yankees he faced on his way to 15 strikeouts in the game, a record at the time. Whitey Ford started for the Yankees and gave up a three run homer to Dodger catcher John Roseboro in the second and trailed 4-0 early.

The Yankees managed just two runs against the masterful Koufax, who pitched a complete game, giving up just six hits, and the Dodgers won 5-2. The Yankees only runs came on a two run homer by left fielder Tom Tresh in the eighth.

In Game number 2, at Yankee Stadium, before 66,455 fans, the Dodgers Johnny Podres bested Yankee starter Al Downing 4-1 with former Yankee Moose Skowron, who was traded to the Dodgers after the 1962 season, hitting a homer for the Dodgers.

The Dodgers got two runs in the top of the first when short stop Maury Wills led off with a single, stole second, went to third on a single by third baseman Jim Gilliam and center fielder Willie Davis then doubled deep to right to score them both and put the Dodgers ahead to stay 2-0.

Game 3 shifted to the west coast in the new Dodger Stadium where 55,912 fans saw one of the better pitching duels of all time between the Dodgers Don Drysdale and the Yankees Jim Bouton.

The Dodgers won 1-0 with the Dodgers limited to just four hits and the Yankees to three. The only run in the contest scored in the first inning when Jim Gilliam singled, went to second on a wild pitch and scored on a single by Tommy Davis. Drysdale pitched a complete game shut out for the win and Boutin went seven innings and got the loss.

The Dodgers completed the four game sweep when Koufax again bested Ford in game four. In front of 55,912 fans, Koufax held the Yankees to one run on six hits while striking our 8 more batters for a total of 23 in two games while Ford gave up only 2 hits and 2 runs in seven innings and took his second loss of the Series.

Yankee Mickey Mantle and Dodger Frank Howard had homered and the was game tied at 1-1 going into the eighth inning. In the Dodger eighth, Gilliam led off with grounder to third but, when the throw from Clete Boyer to Joe Pepitoe at first got away, Gilliam ended up on third. Willie Davis then hit a sacrifice fly to deep center to score Gilliam with the eventual winning run and the Dodgers won the game 2-1 and swept the Yankees in four games.

Koufax was named the Most Valuable Player of the series, pitching 18 innings, giving up only 3 runs and striking out 23 while walking only 3 and throwing 2 complete game wins. In the four games, the Yankees scored just four runs to the Dodgers 12and had managed only 22 hits.

The Yankees streak of World's Championships was stopped at two and it would be 1977 before they would win again. The winning team's individual players' share of the 1963 World Series revenue was just $12,794. and the losers' $7,874. By contrast, in 2012 the winner's share was $377,002. per player and the loser $284,274.

SECTION 29

Barry Bonds won the Most Valuable Player Award in the National League seven times. He won in 1990, 1992, 1993 and 2001, 2002, 2003 and 2004, more times than any other player in baseball history in either league. Nine different players have won the award three times but no other player has won more than three.

LAWRENCE PETER 'YOGI' BERRA

On September 28, 1951, at age 13, I was in Yankee Stadium in New York, with my father, to watch the Yankees play a double header against the Boston Red Sox. The Yankees could clinch the pennant over the second place Cleveland Indians by winning both ends of the double header. At age 13 and a rabid Yankee fan, I could not believe I was there.

Allie Reynolds took the mound for the Yankees in Game 1 of the twin bill. Reynolds was at the top of his game that day. He had already pitched one no hitter that year and had a second no hitter going in the last of the ninth with two outs and the Yankees ahead 8-0. The only person between Reynolds and his second no hitter was the Splendid Splinter Ted Williams, the greatest hitter in baseball at that time and probably of all time.

Reynolds got Williams to hit a pop foul and Yogi Berra got under it and, unbelievably, dropped it. Reynolds went back to the mound and got Williams to hit another pop foul and Yogi caught this one, ending the no hitter and clinching a tie for the pennant for the Yankees.

Five years and ten days later, in Glidden Hall, at Nasson College, in Springvale, Maine, I watched on a black and white television as Don Larsen threw the only perfect game in World Series history against the Brooklyn Dodgers in that same Yankee Stadium. When pinch hitter Dale Mitchell was called out on strikes for the third out of the game, the catcher, that same Yogi Berra, charged the mound and leaped into Larsen's arms and the picture of that happening is one of the most famous pictures in baseball history.

Yogi Berra passed away in 2015 at age 90. The two events above that I was fortunate to have witnessed were just the tip of the iceberg in the amazing career and life of Yogi Berra. Yes, he was perhaps the greatest catcher ever to play the game but he was much more than a catcher.

He was born, May 12, 1925, and raised in The Hill section of St. Louis where he grew up with his friend and fellow catcher Joe Garagiola. After they tried out, together with the Cardinals, Garagiola was signed and Yogi supposedly turned down a contract offer from them because they offered Garagiola more money than they offered him him. Yogi eventually signed with the Yankees.

After just beginning his baseball career with the Class B Norfolk Yankee farm team in 1943, he enlisted in the Navy and trained as a machine gunner on a Rocket Boat and was at Omaha Beach during the D-Day Invasion of Normandy. He returned from the Navy in 1946 and hit .314 in 77 games with the Newark Bears before being brought up to the Yankees in September.

He played for the Yankees from 1946 until 1963. After his playing career was over, he managed the Yankees to a pennant in 1964, managed the Mets from 1972 until 1975, winning the National League pennant in 1973, and managed the Yankees again from 1984 until he was fired by George Steinbrenner after the Yankees started the 1985 season 6-10.

After leaving baseball, he opened the Yogi Berra Museum and Learning Center on the campus of Montclair State University near his home in Montclair, New Jersey. The facility, which, is described in it's literature as capturing 'the rich history of baseball and the career of Yogi Berra is a wonderful learning experience for both adults and students alike', serves thousands annually.

Yogi was almost as well known for his 'Yogi-isms' as for his feats as a baseball player. He is one of the most quoted athletes in the world. My favorite quote supposedly was uttered while he was playing in a baseball game when he was in the Navy and stationed at Groton, Connecticut. After not doing well at his first at bats in a game, swinging at bad pitches, the coach told him to think while he was up there. Yogi supposedly went up and took three strikes without swinging and when he came back to the dug out said 'I can't think and hit at the same time'.

Yogi, the baseball player, was signed by the Yankees in 1943. He played in 14 World Series with the Yankees, 10 of which the Yankees won, from 1947 to 1962, the most of any player in baseball history. He played in a total of 75 World Series games, batting .274 with 12 homers and 39 RBI's. He had a career batting average of .285 and played in a total of 2,120 games and had 2,150 hits, 358 homers and 1,430 RBI's.

He was named to every All Star team from 1948 until 1962 and was Most Valuable Player in the American League in 1951, 1954 and 1955.

He had his greatest year at the plate in 1950, hitting .322 with 28 homers and 124 RBI's. That year was the second year of the Yankees all time record five consecutive World Series wins. He also threw out a remarkable 57.6% of the runners who attempted to steal against the Yankees that year.

Even more impressive is the fact that he was behind the plate in 148 of his team's 154 regular season games that year. He caught more games in 1954, totaling 149. For his career, he batted .285 and hit 358 home runs and drove in 1,430 runs.

He was named to the Hall of Fame in 1972. According to the web site Baseball Reference, the highest salary he earned with the Yankees was $65,000. in 1957. Somehow, I think Yogi would have played for nothing, he loved the game that much.

Yogi passed away on September 22, 2015, exactly 69 years, to the day, after he made his debut as a Yankee in 1946. In that first game of his career, which the Yankees won 4-3 over Connie Mack's Philadelphia Phillies, Yogi, batting eighth, went 2-4 with a home run, two RBI's and a run scored.

Lawrence Peter 'Yogi' Berra was a great player, manager, ambassador and character and a great American. Before his death, he was proposed as a candidate for the Presidential Medal of Freedom and, on November 24, 2015, President Barack Obama awarded him the Medal posthumously.

In the longest game in professional baseball history, 33 innings, between the AAA International League's Pawtucket Red Sox and the Rochester Red Wings, future Hall of Fame Member Cal Ripken, Jr., played third base for the Red Wings and future Hall of Fame Member Wade Boggs played third base for the Red Sox. The game lasted eight hours and twenty-five minutes and there were 882 pitches thrown. The Red Sox won 3-2 when Marty Barrett scored in the last of the 33rd.

HALL OF FAME MANAGERS
TORRE, LARUSSA AND COX

Over the years, the election process for entry into the Baseball Hall of Fame has been the subject of much controversy. The current controversy surrounding the eligibility or electability of players involved with steroid use is just another in a long line of controversies surrounding the election process. Like any other election process in this country a lot of back room politics is involved and sometimes players who should get in don't and some who shouldn't do.

Anyone interested in the history of the Hall of Fame and the manner in which players and others have been elected to or excluded from the Hall should read 'Cooperstown Confidential' by Zev Chafets to get an eye opening look at the process.

No one could complain about the credentials or integrity of the three people elected by the Veteran's Committee in 2013. No one had ever been elected by a unanimous vote of this committee in the past but that year Joe Torre, Bobby Cox and Tony La Russa all were selected on all 16 ballots. The three, all of whom accumulated over 2,000 wins as managers, were well qualified for inclusion in the Hall.

Between them, they had managed the winning team in a total of eight World Series and had taken teams to the Playoffs 45 times. Cox won the World Series with the Braves in 1995, La Russa with the Oakland Athletics of the American League in 1989 and the National League St. Louis Cardinals in 2006 and 2011 and Torre with the Yankees in 1996, 1998, 1999 and 2000.

La Russa retired in 2011 shortly after winning one of the greatest World Series of all time. Two of Torre's World Championship Yankee teams beat Braves teams managed by Bobby Cox in the World Series in 1996 and 1999.

Cox managed the Braves from 1978 until 1981, the Toronto Blue Jays from 1982 to 1985, was General Manager of the Braves from 1986 to 1990 and appointed himself Manager in 1990 and managed until 2010.

Torre managed the Mets from 1977 to 1981, the Braves, (where he succeeded Bobby Cox), from 1982 to 1984, the Cardinals from 1990 to 1995, the Yankees from 1996 to 2007 and the Dodgers from 2008 to 2010. La Russa managed the White Sox from 1979 to 1986, the Athletics from 1987 to 1995 and the Cardinals, from 1996 to 2011.

La Russa managed teams to more victories, 2,728, than anyone in history except Connie Mack and John McGraw. Cox had a total of 2,504 victories, the fourth most in history and Torre was fifth not far behind with 2,236. Collectively, they won a total of 17 league pennants, six each by Torre and La Russa and five by Cox. Cox took teams he managed to the playoffs 16 times, Torre, 15, and La Russa 14.

La Russa was Manager of the Year in 1983 with the Chicago White Sox and with the Oakland Athletics in 1992 and 1998. Cox was Manager of the Year with the Blue Jays in 1985 and with the Braves in 1991, 2004 and 2005 and Torre with the

Yankees in 1996 and 1998. Torre is the only person in Major League history to both play and manage for over 2,000 games.

All three are former Major League players but only Torre of the three had a distinguished career. Cox played third base for the Yankees in 1968 and 1969, playing a total of 220 games and compiling a career batting average of .225.

La Russa, who played second base and shortstop in a career that started in 1963 and lasted until 1971, only appeared in 132 games in that time and hit .199 for his career.

On the other hand, Torre played in 2,209 games as a player with the Braves, Cardinals and Mets from 1960 until 1977. He started as catcher with the Braves, where, as a rookie, he replaced Del Crandall, who was out for the year with an injury, and hit .278. In his second year, with the return of Crandall, Torre was his backup. The next five years, he made the National League All Star Team, the last four as the starting catcher.

In 1969, he was traded to the Cardinals for Orlando Cepeda and, since the Cardinals already had Tim McCarver catching, Torre moved to first base where he hit .289 with 101 RBI's. He was with the Cardinals until 1974 and made the All Star team four more times, as a third baseman. In 1971, he hit .363 and drove in 137 runs and was named the National League's Most Valuable Player. After being traded to the Mets before the 1975 season, he played only 114 games in each of the next two years but hit .306 in 1976. Shortly after being named Mets Player Manager, in 1977, one of the last players to hold that title, he retired to concentrate on managing.

That year's selection committee was made up of eight members of the Hall of Fame, Rod Carew, Carlton Fisk, Whitey Herzog, Tommy Lasorda, Paul Molitar, Joe Morgan, Phil Niekro and Frank Robinson and eight other non-players, four of whom were executives with major league teams and four who represented the baseball media. The committee made its selections from a ballot containing names that were selected by the Historical Overview Committee of the Baseball Writers Association. The ballot that year could only include individuals from baseball's expansion era, from 1973 on. The three were inducted into the Hall of Fame in ceremonies in Cooperstown, NY on June 27, 2014. Coincidentally, Greg Maddux and Tom Glavin, both 300 game winners, who both pitched for Cox in Atlanta, were elected to the Hall on the regular ballot and enshrined along with him at the same ceremony.

Jamie Moyer, a left hander, who pitched in the Major Leagues for 25 years, until he retired at age 49, in 2012, gave up more home runs, 522, in his career than any pitcher in baseball history. Hall of Fame member, right hander, Robin Roberts, gave up the second most homers with 505 in his 19 year career.

TINKER TO EVERS TO CHANCE

These are the saddest of possible words,
"Tinkers to Evers to Chance."
Trio of Bear Cubs and fleeter than birds,
Tinker and Evers and Chance,
Ruthlessly pricking our gonfalon bubble,
Making a Giant hit into a double,
Words that are heavy with nothing but trouble,
"Tinker to Evers to Chance".

These are the words of a poem written by Franklin Pierce Adams, a columnist for the New York Evening Mail, in 1910 to celebrate the Chicago Cubs famed double play combination of Shortstop Joe Tinker, Second Baseman Johnny Evers and First Baseman Frank Chance.

This trio of infielders played for the Cubs from 1902 to 1912 during which time the Cubs won the National League pennant four times, in 1906, 1907, 1908 and 1910.

The poem immortalized a double play combination that completed a total of 54 double plays in 770 games from 1906 through 1910. For you mathematicians in the audience, that is one double play for every 14 plus games, hardly a great accomplishment by today's standards but good enough in those days to get the trio immortalized in poem.

As best I can determine, no one else named Tinker ever played the game of baseball at the Major League level. The word tinker is an interesting one. According to Merriam Webster's Dictionary, the word tinker, used as an intransitive verb, means, among other things, ' … to work with something in an unskilled or insensitive manner. ' We hear it from time to time today when someone refers to someone trying to fix something as tinkering with it, usually in a derogatory sense.

Depending upon who you believe or what you are reading, baseball was invented by Alexander Cartwright, who wrote the first rule book in 1845, or Abner Doubleday, who the Mills Commission in 1908, said invented the game in 1839 at Cooperstown, New York.

Baseball has survived and thrived as our national pastime at least since sometime in the 1800's although there was a by-law in Pittsfield, Massachusetts as early as 1791 that outlawed playing baseball near the Town Hall which would indicate that the game was around even then.

No matter where it was invented and by whom, baseball has survived in almost its original form since sometime in the 1700's or 1800's. Granted, in its infancy as a professional sport, many changes were made. For, example originally if a batted ball was caught on a bounce it was an out, a runner would be called out if a fielder threw the ball and hit or 'plugged' him while he was running. Changes like these made the game what it is today and relatively few changes have been made through the years. The first professional game was supposedly played in Hoboken, New Jersey in 1846.

The game of baseball and the Major Leagues evolved with very little change to the game itself. The Major Leagues have expanded to thirty teams over the years and in 2015 over 73 million fans paid admissions to games, an average of 30,366 per game according to Baseball Amanac, and countless millions others watched or listened on television or radio despite the fact that the game is basically the same as it was fifty or a hundred years ago.

In 2014, professional baseball expanded its instant replay of umpires' calls to include almost every type of play, resulting in the evolution of a game between the umpires and managers where they pretend to be arguing or discussing a call while the manager decides whether to appeal a play or not depending upon what his replay shows.

The same year, a new rule aimed at eliminating collisions at home plate between runners and catchers was put in place to protect the players but the rule was vague and never really defined what blocking the plate meant and the result is less collisions and more confusion.

The same year, a new interpretation of the transfer rule was given umpires to enforce. We have always known that, if a player catches a batted ball before it hits the ground, the batter is out. Similarly, if a player in possession of the ball tags a base for a force out before the runner reaches the base, the runner is out. That is still the case, but the new interpretation said that, if the player drops the ball while transferring it from his glove to his throwing hand the batter or runner shall be safe.

This change led to so much confusion and controversy that, midway through the first month of its implementation it was rescinded and, after much controversy, the rules committee voted to return to the old interpretation of the rule.

Then we have the matter of pitchers applying foreign substances to the ball. The rule is very clear, it is illegal for a pitcher to have or apply a foreign substance to a ball. In April of 2014, he Yankees Michael Pineda was caught with pine tar on his neck while pitching and was ejected and suspended for his actions.

Almost every expert and baseball player quoted in the media say that the use of such substances is common throughout baseball. What did baseball do, immediately began to consider giving pitchers another substance besides the resin bag to apply to the ball legally which will do the same thing the pine tar did for Pineda.

Of course, baseball has been looking at ways of speeding up the game by doing various things since before 2014. One genius even suggested making the games seven innings instead of nine to make for a shorter game.

The argument that the game is too slow and needs to be sped up pales when you look at the attendance figures and the size of the television contracts the teams are signing. The Los Angeles Dodgers averaged 46,479 paid fans per game last year and totaled 3,764,815 paid admissions and they have not been in a World Series since 1988. That plus the total attendance of 73,760,020 does not indicate a fan base with a problem with the length of games or the way they are played.

I would suggest that, when the history of baseball is revised in the future, that the year 2014 be referred to as the Year of the Tinker. Whoever is responsible for that year's attempts to change the game by 'tinkering' with it has certainly gone about it in an 'unskilled and experimental manner'.

SECTION 32

Mariano Rivera, who spent his entire 19 year career with the New York Yankees, holds the record for the most career saves in baseball history, with 652. Trevor Hoffman, who spent most of his 19 year career with the San Diego Padres, has the second highest total saves with 601. No other pitcher has recorded more than 500.

THE GEORGIA PEACH

Tyrus Raymond Cobb, 'The Georgia Peach', was born in Narrows, Georgia, on December 18, 1886. Daniel Ginsburg, of the Sabre Project, in Cobb's biography called him ' .... arguably the greatest player in the history of the game.'

He played the game and lived his life with reckless abandon. His mother shot and killed his father, who Ty had worshiped, and was tried for the killing, during his first seasons in baseball. He himself was charged with attempted murder after a fight with a hotel night watchman in 1909 and the charges were later reduced.

In 1912, he went into the stands and attacked a heckler during a game and was suspended but later reinstated when his teammates rebelled and refused to play unless he was allowed to return. Through all the controversy, he put together year after year of some of the most impressive performances in the history of baseball.

Originally signed by the Augusta team of the South Atlantic, or Sally League, in 1904, he only lasted two games and was released. He played independent ball and did so well that Augusta resigned him in 2005 and he hit .326 in 103 games before being purchased by the Detroit Tigers, for $750., around

August 24 of that year. According to BaseballReference.com, he was paid $1,500. for that season.

He made his debut on August 30 and finished the season with Detroit. The next year, his first full year in the Majors, he hit .316, the lowest average he would have in the next 22 years in Major League baseball. He played his entire career with the exception of a few in the outfield, primarily center field.

He led the Tigers to the American League pennant in 1907, 1908 and 1909, winning the batting title each year with averages of .350, .324 and .377, respectively. He also led the league in hits and runs batted in those three years with 212, 188 and 216 hits and 119, 108 and 107 RBI's. The Tigers lost all three World Series, to the Chicago Cubs in five games in 1907 and 1908 and to the Pittsburgh Pirates, in seven games, in 1909.

These would be the only times Cobb played in the World Series as the Tigers finished as high as second only three times in the rest of his time there and, in the last two years of his career, when he was with the Philadelphia Athletics, they finished second both years.

In his three World Series, he hit only .262, going 17 for 65 with just nine RBI's and seven runs scored in 17 games. His World Series performance was far from typical of his performance at the plate at other times.

Over the 13 year period from 1907 through 1919, he won the American League batting title 12 times, including nine in a row from 1907-1915, and, in the year he did not win it, finished with the second highest average in the league. He never won a batting title after 1919, even though his average was consistently among the highest in the league for the rest of his career. In 1922, he hit .401 and didn't win the title because George Sisler of the St. Louis Browns hit .420.

In 1911, Cobb had hit .420 for his highest average ever and, with his 248 hits and 127 RBI's, won the Most Valuable Player Award for the only time in his career. When comparing his statistics with others who won the MVP Award it would appear that his abrasive personality and all out style of play may have cost him the MVP Award in other years. He hit over .350 16 times in his 24 year career including once when he was over the age of 40.

He was an overly aggressive base runner who often was accused of spiking or trying to spike fielders trying to get him out. Whether that was true or not and it appears that it was, the fact that he stole over fifty bases in a single season nine times in his career, including 96 in 1915, attests to his ability as a base runner. His attitude toward the game was summed up in a quote attributed to him in the Hall of Fame ' I never could stand losing. Second place didn't interest me. I had a fire in my belly.'

He was the Tigers Player/Manager his last six years with the team, from 1921-1926 and his teams had a record of 479 wins and 444 losses during that period, finishing as high as second only once. He retired from the Tigers in 1926 but Connie Mack, the Owner/Manager of the Philadelphia Phillies offered him $50,000. to play for him in 1927, $10,000. more than he ever made with th Tigers and he came back at age 40 and played two years, hitting .357 and .323 in that period.

He hit over .400 three times in his career, in addition to the .420 average in 1911, he hit .409 in 1912 and .401 in 1922. He still holds, and probably will hold the record for the highest career batting average at .366, eight points higher than the great Rogers Hornsby's second place career average of .358.

He was not a home run hitter, although at 6'1' and 175 pounds, he was not small for his era. He had 4,189 hits in his career, second only to Pete Rose's 4,256 but only hit 117 home runs. Although he won the league batting championship and had the highest number of RBI's in four different years, he only won the Triple Crown once when, in 1909, with a league leading batting average of .377 and the highest RBI total of 107, he led the league in homers with just nine, giving him his first and only Triple Crown.

Seven times he led the league in on base percentage and in eight seasons he had the most hits in the league. He also led the league in slugging percentage in eight different seasons.

In addition to the records mentioned above, he ranked second of all time in total singles for a career, with 3,053, fourth in doubles, with 724, second in triples, with 295, second in runs scored, with 2,244, fifth in total bases, with 5,854 and fourth in stolen bases, with 897. He was elected to the Hall of Fame by the Baseball Writer's Association in 1936 with 98.2 % of the vote. He lived to play the game of baseball and only knew one way to play it, to win, no matter what, and he had the ability to go with his desire. As George Sisler, also a Hall of Fame member said ' The greatness of Ty Cobb was something that had to be seen, and to see him was to remember him forever.'

SECTION 33

Babe Ruth had the highest career slugging percentage in baseball history, at .690. Ted Williams was second at .634, Lou Gehrig, third at .632, Jimmie Foxx, the highest and only right handed batter in the top five, fourth at .609 and Barry Bonds, fifth at .607.

THE LEGENDARY SAM FULD

The 2013 Tampa Bay Rays baseball program for opening day and the first home series of the year featured Sam Fuld on the cover and contained a 4 page article about Sam and the problems he has faced and overcome since being diagnosed with type 1 diabetes at the age of 10.

Sam, who was born in Durham, New Hampshire, was an integral part of a Rays team that everyone thought had the potential to make it to the Playoffs again that year.

The Rays did make the playoffs as a Wild Card team that year and beat the Indians in the Wild Card game 4-0 behind Alex Cobb who pitched 6 2/3 innings of shutout ball. Fuld entered the game as a pinch runner, moved to center field in the seventh and right field in the eighth. In his only at bat, he struck out foe the first out in the ninth inning.

In his only appearance in the ALDS, which the Rays lost to the eventual World Series winning Boston Red Sox, three games to one, he ran for James Loney in the eighth inning of Game 3, the only game the Rays won, and scored to put the Rays up 4-3. The Sox tied the game but the Rays won it in the ninth on a walk off homer by Jose Lobaton.

He had been in 119 games for the Rays, batting just .199, with only 176 at bats, while filling in for the regular outfielders often as a late inning defensive replacement.

Not many players from New Hampshire make it to the big time, in fact, in the entire history of baseball, according to the Baseball Almanac, only 50 players have done so. This is due, in large measure, to the weather which limits the baseball season to a much shorter period than milder climates.

This did not deter Sam, who attended Berwick Academy, in Maine, and made the high school team while still in the eighth grade before moving to Phillips Exeter Academy where he was named the New Hampshire Gatorade Player of the Year in 2000.

Sam's parents, Kenneth Fuld, who is Dean of the College of Liberal Arts at UNH and his mother, Amanda Merrill, a State Senator in New Hampshire, are rightly proud of what their son has accomplished. The Rays program quoted his father as saying 'I'm as proud of the way that he's dealt with his diabetes as I am with his baseball accomplishments.'

After High School, Sam attended Stamford University, where he was named a first team All American twice. He was drafted by the Chicago Cubs after his Junior year but opted to finish his education and college baseball career instead of signing. At Stamford, in addition to his All American recognition, he set a career record for the most hits by a player in the College World Series.

He was drafted again by the Cubs at the end of his Senior year and signed with them. He was an All Star in the Florida State League his first year in organized ball and Most Valuable Player in the Arizona Fall League in 2007. Despite being called up to the Cubs in late season three years running, Sam only started 40 big league games during that time.

After the 2010 season, Sam was traded to Tampa Bay and played in 105 games for the Rays hitting just .240 in 2011 but becoming a fan favorite mostly due to the all out effort he puts into every part of the game and his ability to make sensational catches in the outfield. Late in the season, he suffered a wrist injury which required surgery and kept him on the disabled list for much of 2012. He only played in 44 games and hit .255 that year.

The Tampa Bay Rays baseball program listed Sam as 5'10' and 175 pounds. Actually, Sam is probably closer to 5'8" and 160 pounds than to the listed sizes. That lack of size, however, did not keep him from being an asset to the Rays, both offensively and defensively.

His seemingly impossible catches earned him many nicknames with fans and fellow players, among them 'The Legendary Sam Fuld' and 'Super Sam'. His page on MLB.com shows a picture of him diving for a ball in the outfield which is typical of his all out style of play.

I was in Tropicana Field for the Rays Opening Day that year and Sam started in left field and batted second in the Rays lineup. In the eighth inning, with the bases full of Orioles and 2 outs, Adam Jones, the Orioles center fielder, who already had three hits in the game, hit a sinking line drive to left. Most outfielders would have played the ball on one hop and tried to limit the damage but Sam charged the ball at full speed and made a sliding catch on his back just before the ball hit the ground to end the inning.

In addition to his baseball accomplishments, Sam has founded the Sam Fuld Diabetes Camp, a baseball camp for youngsters suffering from diabetes. With all Sam has been through since his diabetes diagnosis, the constant monitoring of blood levels and injections, Sam has committed himself to helping other youngsters who are experiencing the same problems.

Sitting in the ballpark the first three games of that season, it was pretty obvious to me that, even though it looked like, although Sam would be the fourth outfielder that year rather than a starter, he was, along with David Price, the Cy Young winning pitcher, the fan favorite in Tampa.

At the end of the 2013 season, Sam was a Free Agent and signed with the Oakland Athletics on February 4, 2014. He was claimed off waivers from the A's by the Minnesota Twins on April 20 of that year and, on July 31, 2014, after hitting .274 in 53 games was traded back to Oakland for Tommy Milone.

He hit .209 for Oakland the rest of the way in 60 games. Oakland made the playoffs as a Wild Card but lost to eventual American League Winner Kansas City in the Wild Card game, 9-8, in 12 innings. Fuld batted second and went 2-5, scoring a run, playing center and moving to right later in the game in a losing cause.

In 2015, he hit just .197 in 120 games and was used as a defensive replacement often. He had seven outfield assists in his limited play, fourth highest in the league. He is expected to compete for a starting spot in the A's outfield in spring training in 2016.

As his Manager in Tampa Bay, Joe Maddon, said of Sam in the team program in 2013, ' There's an identification that draws the average fan to him. In addition, there's the energy with which he plays that's attractive. The average fan loves to see the way Sam Fuld plays the game. And then finally there's the fact that he's had so much to overcome with the diabetes. And he's bright, too. When people look under the surface a little bit and see all these different components, he's easy to identify with and root for. '

Sam Fuld is not only fun to watch play baseball but is also an inspiration to those who recognize the handicaps he has overcome to get where he is today, in his ninth year as a Major Leaguer.

Bobo Holloman of the St. Louis Browns was the only pitcher in baseball history to throw a no hitter in his first start. He did it on May 6, 1953, against the Philadelphia Athletics. Only Wilson Alvarez, of the Washington Senators, who no hit the Baltimore Orioles on August 11, 1991 and Clay Buchholz, of the Boston Red Sox, who also no hit Baltimore, on September 1, 2007, pitched a no hitter in their second start.

THE 1916 WORLD SERIES

In 1916 the Boston Red Sox won the pennant and faced the Brooklyn Robins in the World Series. The Sox had won 91 and lost 63 during the season to edge the Chicago White Sox by two games for the American League crown. The Robins at 94-60 had beaten the Philadelphia Phillies by 2 ½ games in the National. This was the Red Sox third trip to the Series in five years.

Both leagues were made up of eight teams in one division in 1916. In each division, there were five teams that are still playing under the same name, in the same league, in the same city, 100 years later in 2016. Those teams are the Boston Red Sox, Chicago White Sox, Detroit Tigers, New York Yankees and Cleveland Indians in the American League and the Philadelphia Phillies, Chicago Cubs, Pittsburgh Pirates, St. Louis Cardinals and Cincinnati Reds in the National League.

In Game 1, of the 1916 World Series, played at Braves Field before 36,117 fans, Ernie Shore started for the Red Sox and had a 6-1 lead going into the ninth inning. Robins first baseman Jake Daubert walked to lead off the inning and right fielder Casey Stengel singled to right. Left fielder Zach Wheat then bounced back to Shore who got the force at third for the first out. Shore then hit second baseman George Cutshaw with a pitch to load the bases. Third baseman Mike Mowrey then grounded to second and, when the ball was misplayed by second baseman Hal Janvrin, Stengel and Wheat both scored making it 6-3.

Short stop Ivy Olson got an infield single to load the bases and catcher Chief Meyers popped to first for the second out. Fred Merkle, batting for the pitcher, walked to force in Olson and make it 6-4. Carl Mays was brought in to relieve Shore and gave up a single to center fielder Hi Myers scoring Mowrey to mae it 6-5. Mays then got Daubert to ground out to short for the final out and the Sox had held on and won Game 1, 6-5.

Game 2, at Braves Field, featured Babe Ruth pitching for the Red Sox against Sherry Smith for the Robins with 47,373 fans on hand. The game went into the 14th inning tied 1-1. In the first, with two outs Hi Myers hit an inside the park homer for the Robins and the Sox came back with one in the third when short stop Everett Scott tripled and scored when Ruth grounded to second.

In the fourteenth, Sox first baseman Dick Hoblitzell walked and left fielder Duffy Lewis sacrificed him to second. Mike McNally ran for Hoblitzell and scored when pinch hitter Del Gainer singled to left for the win. After giving up the run in the first, Ruth threw 13 1/3 scoreless innings to start his streak of 29 2/3 consecutive scoreless World Series innings which he completed two years later against the Cubs. That record stood until the Yankees Whitey Ford broke it in 1961.

In Game 3, Colby Jack Coombs, from Waterville, Maine, and Colby College, started on the mound for the Robins. The Robins got one run in the third on an RBI single by Cutshaw and the pitcher Coombs singled another in in the fourth. In the fifth, Olson got a two run triple and the Robins were up 4-0.

The Sox came back with two runs in the sixth when pinch hitter

Olaf Henricksen walked and scored on right fielder Harry Hooper's triple to right. Center fielder Chick Shorter then singled in Hooper to make it 4-2. Gardner homered for the Sox in the seventh but then Jeff Pfeffer shut out the Sox the last two innings and the final was 4-2, Robins, and the Series was 2-1, Boston. Coombs got the win for the Robins. A crowd of just 21,087 were on hand in little Ebbets Field.

Dutch Leonard started Game 4, in Brooklyn, for the Sox and gave up two runs in the first when right fielder Jimmy Johnston led off with a triple and scored when Hi Myers singled to right. Myers scored on an error and the Robins were up, 2-0. In the Sox second Hoblitzell walked, Lewis doubled to right and Gardner hit a long homer to left center and the Red Sox were up 3-2.

Boston added single runs in the fourth, fifth and seventh and Leonard shut the Robins off after the two in the first as the Sox took Game 4, 6-2. Leonard pitched a complete game five hitter for the win while Rube Marquard, who went just four innings, for the Robins, giving up four runs, got the loss. A crowd of 21,662 was on hand for the game as the Sox went up three games to one.

The Robins got out to a quick lead in the second inning of Game 5, back in Boston, scoring against starter Ernie Shore when Cutshaw walked, was sacrificed to second, went to third on a ground out and scored on a passed ball to make it 1-0, Robins. The Sox came right back to tie it at 1-1 in their half of the second when Lewis tripled to left and scored on a sacrifice fly by Gardner.

In the Sox half of the third, catcher Hick Cady singled to right and Hooper walked. Janvrin then reached on a ground ball error and Cady scored. Shorten then singled to center to score Hooper and the Sox were up, 3-1. They added a run in the fifth when Hooper singled to right and scored on Janvrin's long double to center. That was to be the end of the scoring for the day.

Meantime, Shore was shutting the Robins down, going the route and giving up just the one unearned run on three hits for his second win of the series.

The Sox had won their third World Series in five years, winning in 1912, 1915 and 1916 and would win again in 1918, defeating the Chicago Cubs four games to two. The Boston Braves had won the World Series in 1914, giving Boston the World Series winner in four of five seasons. After 1918, as all Red Sox fans know, whether due to the Curse of the Bambino or not, the Sox did not win the World Series again until 2004, 86 years later.

Yankee second baseman, Bobby Richardson, holds the record for the most runs batted in in a single World Series with 12 in the 1960 Series when he won the MVP Award. He is tied with Marty Barrett and Lou Brock for the most hits in a single World Series, 13, in the 1964 Series. A .266 career hitter, he hit .305 in seven World Series.

WHY DO CATCHERS BECOME MANAGERS?

Joe Girardi, Mike Scoscia, Mike Matheny, Kevin Cash, Bruce Bochy, Ned Yost, Bob Melvin, Brad Ausmus, A. J. Hinch, Scott Servais, Jeff Banister and John Gibbons and are all Major League Baseball Managers. What else do they all have in common? If you guessed that they all were catchers during their Major League playing careers, you are right.

Now, how about this one? Joe Maddon and Fredi Gonzalez are both Major League Baseball Managers. What else do they have in common? They are all former Minor League baseball players who never made it to the Major Leagues as players but spent their playing careers as catchers.

There are thirty Major League Baseball teams with thirty managers. Going into the 2016 season, fourteen of those managers were former catchers. Why are fourteen of the thirty managers people whose baseball experience was obtained as a catcher? After all, catch is only one of the nine positions on the field at any given time, yet 47% of the Managers come from the ranks of catchers.

What special ability required to manage a baseball team does a player glean from playing at this unglamorous position that gives him the skills to be a manager? After all, the catcher's equipment has always been referred to as the 'Tools of Ignorance'. One wouldn't think that ignorance would be an asset in such a complex position. According to BaseballReference.com, the reference to the tools of ignorance was ' ...meant to be ironic, contrasting the intelligence needed by a catcher to handle the duties of the position with the foolishness needed to play a position hazardous enough to require so much protective equipment.'

The catcher takes a position, generally more than one hundred times in the average ball game, squatting behind the batter, that puts him at severe risk. Both ball and bat are moving at a speed around 100 miles per hour and arrive at a spot directly in front of the catcher at precisely the same instant. If you have never experienced the sensation when this happens, then you don't have a true appreciation of the meaning of the phrase 'in the blink of an eye'.

In addition to these hazards, the catcher is the only player on the field that it used to be acceptable to crash into while running full speed into home plate. He is an advocate for the pitcher in ball and strike counts, making him a favorite target of umpires. If an opposing batter gets hit with a pitch, the catcher, who obviously must have called the bean ball, is the most logical target for the opposition's pitcher to get even against.

Given the dangers involved and the options available, why would any sane person choose to catch? While catching is one of the most dangerous occupations on any sports field, it's where the action is. The catcher is involved in every play. Every play starts with a pitch which the catcher calls by signaling to the pitcher what to throw and where to throw it.

While following general directions, given by signs from the dugout, the catcher must consider a myriad of things while deciding, in a few seconds, which pitch he will call for next. Among the things he must consider are the ability, condition, mental attitude and performance so far that day of his pitcher who, by the way, is only one of 11 or 12 different pitchers he may catch this week, the situation on the field, including the ball and strike count, the number of outs, the score, any base runners and their locations, speed and ability and, of course, the batter, including, but not limited to his ability, physical condition, what he has seen in previous at bats and what he can be expected to want to accomplish this at bat.

I have merely scraped the surface of the things a catcher must anticipate in this situation. Most of us would need a computer to catalog the things we would need to consider before putting down those fingers to call for the pitch, never mind analyze those factors and come up with a decision.

Once the ball leaves the pitcher's hand, the real action begins. This person squatting on his haunches behind home plate who was just imitating a rocket scientist without a computer now becomes an amazing specimen of human agility and reaction. The pitch may come in at anywhere between 60 and 100 miles per hour, may go where it was supposed to go or somewhere else and may not even be the pitch the catcher thought he called for. If you have ever expected an 80 mile per hour curve and gotten a 100 mile per hour fast ball you know where the term handcuffed came from.

Assuming the ball is not put in play, which it isn't most of the time, and the catcher catches it and there is no one trying to steal a base, the scenario starts all over again, starting from the signal from the bench. If the ball is hit, depending upon where it is hit and whether it is caught or one of the other dozens of things that can happen, the catcher now has other responsibilities. These include backing up first base on grounders, directing throws within the infield, preparing to catch a ball for a play at the plate and on and on and on. After this play is over, his responsibilities begin again.

Considering their responsibilities and all they have to learn to play their position, is it surprising that catchers make good managers? The catcher is like the football quarterback, who must know the role of each player in every play. That is why catchers make the best managers and why 47 percent of Major League Baseball Managers are former catchers.

Yankee center fielder Mickey Mantle holds the career record for most World Series home runs with 18. Yankees Babe Ruth and Yogi Berra are second and third with 15 and 12, respectively. Brooklyn Dodger great Duke Snider is fourth with 11.

ROGER CLEMENS

Roger Clemens won the Cy Young Award seven times, with four different teams, in two different leagues. He won it in the American League six times, three times with the Boston Red Sox, twice with the Toronto Blue Jays, once with the New York Yankees and, once in the National League with the Houston Astros. Randy Johnson is the only pitcher to win it five times and Greg Maddux and Steve Carlton are the only two to win it four times.

Clemens was chosen in the 12th round of the 1981 draft by the New York Mets but elected to stay in college. In 1983, he was drafted in the first round by the Boston Red Sox and signed with them on June 21, 1983.

He started at Winter Haven in the Class A Florida League that year and went 3-1 there with a 1.24 ERA before being moved up to New Britain in the AA Eastern League where he won 4 and lost 1 with a 1.38 ERA and had 59 strike outs in just 52 innings. He started 1984 at Pawtucket in the AAA International League before being brought up to the parent team where he made his debut on May 15, 1984.

In that first game, Roger started and lasted just 5 2/3 innings against the Indians, in Cleveland, giving up five runs, four earned, on 11 hits. Not an auspicious debut for a pitcher, who, over the next 13 years, would win 192 games and lose just 111 for the Sox, while posting an ERA of 3.06 and winning the Cy Young Award three times.

In 1986, he led the Sox to the American League pennant, winning 20 and losing just 4, with a 2.48 ERA. He was named Major League Player of the Year, American League MVP and Cy Young Award winner and was the MVP in the All Star Game. The Sox lost the Series to the New York Mets and Clemens started Game 2 but lasted just 4 1/3 innings, giving up three runs on five hits in a game the Sox won, 9-3. He started Game 6 and pitched seven innings, giving up just one earned run on four hits but the Sox blew the game in the tenth.

In 1987, he won the Cy Young again going 20-9 with a 2.97 ERA, 18 complete games and seven shutouts. In 1990, he won 21 and lost just 6 with a 1.93 ERA but lost the Cy Young Award, coming in second behind Bob Welch of the American League Champion Oakland A's who won 27 while losing 6 with a 2.95 ERA. In 1991, with a record of 18-10 and an ERA of 2.62, he won his third Cy Young Award.

From 1991-1995, he won 66 and lost 47. In 1995 the Sox won the Eastern Division title but were swept in the ALDS by Cleveland. Clemens pitched the first game of the series, going seven innings and giving up three runs but had no decision as the Sox lost in extra innings.

In 1996, after probably his worst year in baseball, when he won 10 and lost 13 with a 3.63 ERA, for a Red Sox team that finished in third place, he was granted Free Agency. On December 13, he signed with the Toronto Blue Jays for $8.4 million and proceeded to have two spectacular years, winning 21 and losing 7 with a 2.05 ERA and striking out 292 in 1997 and winning 20 and losing 6 with a 2.65 ERA and 271 strikeouts in 1998. He won the Cy Young Award and the pitching Triple Crown both years for a team that won 164 and lost 160 and finished in 3rd and 5th places those years.

After that performance, Toronto traded him to the New York Yankees on February 18, 1999, for Homer Bush, Graeme Lloyd and David Wells. In his first two years with the Yankees, at ages 35 and 36, he won a total of 27 and lost 18. In 1999, the Yankees won the American League pennant and swept the Atlanta Braves in the World Series. Roger started Game 4, pitching 7 2/3 innings and giving up just one run as the Yankees clinched the sweep, winning 4-1.

In 2000, the Yankees won the pennant and faced the New York Mets in the Subway Series. The Yankees won the Series, four games to one, and Clemens held the Mets to two hits and no runs for eight innings, of Game 2, leaving ahead 6-0. Jeff Nelson and Mariano Rivera, in relief of Clemens, gave up five runs in the ninth but they managed to stop the bleeding at 6-5 and Clemens got the win.

In 2001, he won 20 and lost just 3, while posting a 3.51 ERA and won his sixth Cy Young Award. The Yankees won the pennant for the third year in a row but lost the World Series to the Arizona Diamondbacks in seven games. Clemens started Game 3, went 7 1/3 innings, giving up one run on three hits and striking out 9, for the win as the Yankees won 2-1. He started Game 7 and pitched 6 1/3 innings, giving up just one run on seven hits and striking out 10, leaving tied at 1-1 in a game that the great Mariano River would blow in the last of the ninth to give the Diamondbacks the Series.

Over the next two years with the Yankees, he won 30 and lost 15. In 2002, they won the American League East but lost in the first round to the Anaheim Angels. Clemens pitched Game 1, giving up four runs and leaving with the game tied 4-4 in a game the Yankees eventually won.

In 2003, they won the pennant again and faced the Florida Marlins in the Series. Clemens started and went seven innings in

Game 4, giving up three runs and leaving behind in a game the Yankee eventually lost in 12 innings 4-3. The Marlins won the Series four games to two.

After the 2003 season he became a Free Agent, at age 41, and signed with the Houston Astros of the National League. In 2004, his first year with the Astros, he won his seventh Cy Young Award with a record of 18-4 and a 2.98 ERA.

The next year, 2005, the Astros won the National League pennant and he won 13 and lost 8 with a 1.87 ERA, the best in the league at age 42. In the World Series, against the Chicago White Sox, he started Game 1 but only lasted two innings, giving up three runs on four hits. It was his only appearance of the series as the Astros were swept by the Sox. In 2006, he went 7-6 with a 2.30 ERA.

At the end of that season, he became a Free Agent again and signed with the Yankees on May 6, 2007. He started 17 games for the Yankees and won six and lost six with a 4.18 ERA. In December of 2007, he was made a Free Agent by the Yankees and retired from baseball.

In his remarkable 24 year career, he won 354 games, ninth most in history, and lost just 184 with a 3.12 ERA. He pitched 118 complete games, including 46 shutouts. His 4,672 strikeouts are the third highest total by any player in history. In addition to his seven Cy Young Awards and the others awards mentioned in this article, he was named to the All Star Team 11 times, led the American League in ERA six times, in strikeouts five times and wins four times. In post season play he won 12 and lost 8, with a 3.75 ERA, including winning three games without a loss while posting a 2.37 ERA in six World Series.

Carlton Fisk hit more home runs after the age of 40 than any other player in baseball history. He had 72. Darrell Evans was second with 67 and Barry Bonds and David Winfield are tied for third with 59.

THE 2011 ST. LOUIS CARDINALS

The 2011 St. Louis Cardinals had led the National League Central Division for most of the first half of the season, falling out of first on July 27 and never regaining the Division lead. They were, in second place, 10 ½ games behind the Milwaukee Brewers on September 5 and had a five game lead on the third place Cincinnati Reds.

Only the second place team with the best record in each league would qualify for the Wild Card and make the playoffs that year. With only 21 games left, it did not appear that the Cards could catch the Brewers so it looked like a Wild Card berth was their only chance to make the Playoffs. They were tied with the San Fancisco Giants, the second place team in the Western Division, with identical 74-67 records but were 8 ½ games behind Atlanta, in second in the East with an 82-58 record on that date.

The Cards put together a streak and won 15 of the next 20 games while the Braves were losing 14 of 21 and the teams were tied for the Wild Card spot with 89-72 records going into the last day of the season. The Cards were playing the last place Houston Astros and the Braves were playing the first place Philadelphia Phillies, who had already clinched the pennant.

The Cardinals put together a 12 hit attack to beat the Astros, 8-0, behind Chris Carpenter's complete game two hit shutout. The Braves led 3-2 going to the top of the ninth but blew the lead and the game in the 13th, 4-3. As improbable as that comeback was, it would only get better for Cardinals fans. The Cards would meet the Phillies in the Division Series.

They split two games at Philadelphia, the Phils won 11-6 and the Cards 5-4 to go to St. Louis tied. They also split in St. Louis, with the Phils winning Game 3, 3-2 and the Cards Game 4, 5-3, to go to Game 5, in Philadelphia, tied two games each. In the deciding game, Roy Halladay started for Philadelphia and Chris Carpenter for the Cards.

Short stop Raphael Furcal led off the Cardinals first with a long triple to center and center fielder Skip Schumaker lined a double to right and it was 1-0 Cardinals. That was the scoring for the day as Carpenter pitched another complete game shut out, holding the Phils to three hits, not allowing a hit after the sixth and the Cardinals had dodged another bullet and were on the way to the League Championship Series. Halladay went eight innings, allowing just four more hits while holding the Cards at 1-0.

In the League Championship Series, the Cardinals faced the Milwaukee Brewers, who had beaten the Cards by six games during the regular season in the Central Division. The Brewers won Game 1 at Milwaukee, 9-6, and the Cards pounded out 17 hits to take Game 2, 12-3. The teams went to St. Louis tied at one apiece and the Cards won Game 3, with Chris Carpenter getting the win, 4-3. The Brewers won Game 4, 4-2, but the Cards came back to win Game 5, 7-1, and the teams returned to Milwaukee for Game 6 with the Cards up 3-2.

In Game 6, the Cards got four in the first, the big hit a three run homer by third baseman David Freese, his third homer of the Series, one in the second on a solo homer by Furcal, and four more in the third including a lead off homer by first baseman Albert Pujols, to lead 9-4 after three innings and win 12-6 to earn a trip to the World Series. Freese, who had 12 hits in 22 at bats, a .545 average, with nine RBI's and seven runs scored with his three home runs, was the Series MVP.

In Game 1, at St. Louis, it was tied 2-2 going to the last of the sixth, and Freese doubled and scored when Alan Craig, batting for starter Chris Carpenter, singled, off Alexi Ogando, making it 3-2 and it stayed that way. Jason Motte got the Rangers 1-2-3 in the top of the ninth and the Cards were up 1-0.

Game 2 was another pitcher's duel, scoreless through six. In the seventh, Freese and Nick Punto singled and Freese moved to third. Ogando came in to pitch for the second day in a row with Allen Craig pinch hitting for the pitcher. Craig singled again to drive in Freese again and it was 1-0.

It went that way until the top of the ninth when, with Jason Motte in in relief for the Cards, Kinsler reached on a pop fly single and stole second. Elvis Andrus singled and went to second on an error. Scott Hamilton his a sac fly to right to score Kinsler and Andrus went to third. Michael Young then hit a sac fly to center and the Rangers were up 2-1. Neftali Feliz came on to pitch for Texas in the last of the ninth and, after walking catcher Yadier Molina, shut the Cards down and the Rangers won 2-1 and it was a 1-1 series going to Texas.

The Cardinals won a slug fest in Game 3, scoring 16 runs on 15 hits and winning 16-7. The Rangers tied it at two games apiece, winning Game 4, 4-0, the big hit a three run homer by catcher Mike Napoli in the Rangers sixth.

Game 5 was a rematch of Game 1, with Chris Carpenter facing C. J. Wilson. Wilson left behind 2-1 in the top of the sixth and Adrian Beltre homered to tie the game in the bottom of the inning. In the Rangers eighth, Young doubled and, with one out, Nelson Cruz was walked intentionally. Marc Rzepczynski replaced Carpenter and gave up an infield single to David Murphy to load the bases. Mike Napoli then doubled to center to score Young and Cruz with what turned out to be the winning runs.

Down three games to two, the Cards went back home facing elimination. In Game 6, both teams had their hitting shoes on and it was 4-4 after six innings. In the seventh, Texas got back to back homers from Beltran and Cruz and Kinsler drove in another run to make it 7-4. Craig homered for the Cards in the eighth and the Cards went to the last of the ninth behind, 7-5. Pujols doubled and Berkman walked with one out. Craig struck out for out number two and the Cards were down to their last out again. David Freese then hit a long fly over Nelson Cruz's head in right for a triple and it was tied again and going to the tenth.

In the top of the tenth, Andrus singled and Hamilton homered and the Cards were down two, again. To start the last of the tenth, Daniel Descalso and John Jay singled and were sacrificed to second. With one out, Ryan Theriot grounded out to third and Descalso scored but two were out. Berkman came through with single to center, scoring Jay and the Cards had dodged another bullet.

Jake Westbrook shut the Rangers down in the 11th and the Cardinals came up in the last of the 11th with, guess who, David Freese. Mark Lowe came in in relief for the Rangers and, with the count 3-2, Freese homered and the Cardinals had done it again and were headed for Game 7, at home.

Game 7 was almost anticlimactic after the excitement of the Playoffs and Series. Texas got two runs in the first when Andrus walked and Hamilton and Young hit back to back doubles but the Cards came back with two in the bottom half when, with two outs, again, Pujols and Berkman walked and Freese doubled to drive them in.

Craig homered in the third and, in the fifth, with the Cardinals bases loaded, a walk and a hit batter forced in two more. The Cards added another in the seventh but Chris Carpenter and four relievers shut down the Rangers after the first inning and the Cardinals had held on to win the Series.

David Freese, who went 8-23 with seven RBI's and four runs scored, was MVP of the Series. It was one of the most exciting season finishes, Playoff and World Series runs ever.

SECTION 38

The New York Yankees' Yogi Berra holds the record for the most World Series appearances as a member of the winning team with 10. His teammate, Joe DiMaggio is second with nine and four other Yankees, Bill Dickey, Phil Rizzuto, Frankie Crosetti and Lou Gehrig are tied for third with nine each. Crosetti is the only one of the six who has not been elected to the Hall of Fame.

JAMIE MOYER

Jamie Moyer pitched and won the 269th game of his baseball career on May 16, 2012. In that same game, he also drove in two runs when he beat out a weak ground ball to the right side with runners on second and third and both runners scored. Jamie Moyer was born on November 18, 1962 and was 49 years, 5 months and 29 days old on that day, making him the oldest pitcher in baseball history to win a game and the oldest batter in baseball history to drive in a run.

He was born in Sellersvile, Pennsylvania, and, after pitching at St. Joseph University and winning 16 games with a 1.99 ERA, in 1984, was drafted by the Chicago Cubs in the sixth round of that year's draft. After two years in the minor leagues, he made his debut with the Cubs on June 7, 1986 against the Philadelphia Phillies, starting and throwing 6 1/3 innings, giving up four runs, three earned, on eight hits and getting the win. He would go 5-6 that year.

He would pitch 26 years in the Major Leagues, playing for eight different teams, four in the American League, The Seattle Mariners, Baltimore Orioles, Texas Rangers and Boston Red Sox and four in the National League, the Cubs, Philadelphia Phillies,

St. Louis Cardinals and Colorado Rockies. He spent the most time, 11 years, in Seattle and won 145 while losing 87 there.

At 6' 1" and 170 pounds, the right hander was never a hard thrower, relying on pin point control and change of speed to get by. In his last year in baseball, with the Colorado Rockies, I watched him pitch in Spring Training and his fast ball was in the low to mid eighties, yet he still pitched five innings against his old team, the Mariners, giving up just one run and striking out five batters. His mound opponent that day was Felix Hernandez who was born the year Jamie made his Major League debut.

He won 20 or more games twice in his career. In 2001, at age 38, with the Mariners, he was 20-6 with a 3.43 ERA in 33 starts. The Mariners won the Western Division that year and faced the Cleveland Indians in the ALDS. Jamie started and won games 2 and 5, going six innings and giving up one run on five hits in Game 2 and pitching six innings and giving up one run on three hits in Game 5. Against the Yankees, he pitched and won the third game, the only game the Mariners won, as they lost the series 4-1, lasting seven innings and giving up two runs on four hits.

In 2003, at age 40, he won 21 and lost seven, with a 3.27 ERA, for the Mariners and made the All Star team for the only time in his career. In 2008, at age 45, pitching for the Philadelphia Phillies, he made his first and only appearance in the World Series after compiling a 16-7 record with a 3.71 ERA in the regular season. In Game 3 of that World Series, the 45 year old started against the Tampa Bay Rays and went 6 1/3 innings, leaving with his team ahead 4-2 in a game the Phils eventually won on a walk off hit in the 9th inning.

In 2010, at age 47, he was 9-9 with the Phillies when he suffered an elbow injury, in July, after 19 starts, and had to have Tommy John surgery. Everyone assumed that his career was finally over. He was out of baseball for the entire 2011 season. Over the winter that year, the Colorado Rockies invited him to come as a non roster invitee for a tryout in Spring Training. He surprised everyone in Spring Training and not only made the team but was given the start in Game 2 of the regular season.

He was 2-5 with the Rockies with a 5.70 ERA when they released him on June 4, 2012, five months and two weeks before his fiftieth birthday. Even then, Jamie Moyer didn't go quietly. The Baltimore Orioles signed him as a Free Agent on June 6, two days later, and, after two starts with their Norfolk team in the AAA International League, where he won one and lost one, they released him on June 23.

Two days later, on June 25, the Toronto Blue Jays signed him as a Free Agent and, after two starts with their Las Vegas team in the AAA Pacific Coast League, where he went 1-1, they released him on July 16.

At the age of 49, he finally called it quits after one of the most remarkable careers in baseball history. For a pitcher who they always joked could not break a pane of glass with his fastball, Jamie Moyer had quite a run. He won 269 games and lost 209 with a career 4.25 ERA. His 269 wins are the 26th most by any pitcher in baseball history. His 638 games started is the 16th most in baseball history and his 4,074 innings pitched the 40th most in baseball history. Another record, and probably one he'd probably rather forget, he gave up more home runs, 522, than any one in history.

Jamie Moyer was never a famous name that everyone recognized but chances are that his records as the oldest pitcher ever to win a game and the oldest hitter ever to drive in a run will never be broken.

SECTION 39

Andy Pettitte holds the record for the most post season games, including Playoffs and World Series Games, won by a pitcher with 19 wins. John Smolz is second with 15, Tommy Glavine third with 14 and Roger Clemens fourth with 12.

1971 TICKET PRICES

I recently came across a Boston Red Sox home schedule for the 1971 season, complete with a schedule of prices for seats in Fenway. I know the first thought that crossed your mind when you read that. I wonder how much tickets cost in those days.

I hope you are sitting down when you read this because if you wanted to sit in a box seat at Fenway Park in 1971, it cost the huge sum of $3.75. If you were willing to sit in the bleachers, a seat was $1.00. A general admission seat was $1.50 and reserved seats were $2.75. There were no special prices for games with 'premium' teams. All regular season games were priced equally.

That year, there were still two divisions in each league with six teams in each division. The Eastern Division contained the Sox, Yankees and Orioles but Tampa Bay and Toronto had not been added yet. The other three teams were the Tigers, Indians and Washington Senators. The Western Division was made up of the Athletics, Royals, White Sox, Angels, Twins and Brewers.

On May 31 of that year, if you bought a ticket to see the Red Sox play Kansas City, you were treated to something you'll never see today or in the future, two games for the price of one. There was actually a double header built in to the schedule. Not a double admission twi-nighter caused by a rainout, but a real two-fer, one admission got you two games. If you followed the Sox on the road, you could get the same deal against the White Sox in Chicago on August 1 and, believe it or not, you could see the Yankees and Red Sox in a twin bill on September 6 in Yankee Stadium.

Just for the fun of it, I did a little research and found that the Sox did not fold down the stretch as they did many years around that time. The folks of Red Sox Nation, although the Nation had not officially been founded then, had to settle for a third place finish though, winning a grand total of 85 games. All was not lost however as the hated Yankees finished in fourth with only 82 wins.

That Baltimore Oriole team that barely made the .500 mark in 2015, 44 years later, won the eastern division in 1971 with 101 wins and 61 losses while the Oakland Athletics won the Western Division with the same record. Interestingly enough, the Eastern Division had four teams over .500 while the Western Division had only two. I guess, even in 1971, the Eastern Division was the stronger.

In the National League, the Pittsburgh Pirates won the East with 97 wins and the San Francisco Giants limped in to win the West with 90 wins.

With two divisions of six teams in each league, there were no wild card teams in the mix so the Division Winners played for the right to play in the World Series. Baltimore got by Oakland in the American League and the Pirates beat out San Francisco for the National League pennant.

The World Series began in Baltimore with Baltimore winning the first game, 5-3, with Dave McNally getting the win. The Orioles coasted behind Jim Palmer in game number 2, winning 11-3.

The scene then shifted to Pittsburgh where the Pirates won game number 3 by a score of 5-1 with Steve Blass the winner. Game 4 saw the Pirates even the series at two games each with a 4-3 win.

In game 5, Nelson Briles shut out the Orioles 4-0 while Dave McNally started and took the loss for the Orioles.

The scene shifted back to Baltimore where McNally, having lost the day before, came in in relief in Game 6 and won the game in the tenth inning 3-2 to send the series to the seventh game.

The seventh game was another thriller, won by Pittsburgh 2-1 behind Steve Blass who pitched another standout game. The great Roberto Clemente hit a home run which was critical to the Pirates win. Clemente, who would get his 3,000th hit the next year before dying in a plane crash in December, was named the series Most Valuable Player.

Forty-five years later, in 2016, prices in Fenway Park, a field box seat costs from $135. to $180. depending upon opponent and bleacher seats from $28. to $42. for a single game. In 1971, you could have seen every game of the season at Fenway from a box seat for $222.75 or from the bleachers for a total expenditure of $81.

Despite the increased cost, Fenway Park and baseball overall continues to see increases or very slight decreases in attendance annually and dramatically increased television revenues with no end in sight. With revenue sharing and the expanded wild card system keeping more teams in the pennant chases later into the season, chances are the attendance will increase or at least remain stable.

If the difference in price between 1971 and 2016 has not hurt attendance and revenues yet, it is obvious that baseball fans will find a way to get their baseball 'fix' regardless of the cost.

The player's strike, which began on August 12, 1994, and lasted 232 days until it ended on April 2, 1995, caused the cancellation of 948 games. Because of the strike, most teams played 113 games in 1994, there was no World Series and the 1995 season was just 144 games long.

STAN 'THE MAN' MUSIAL

Stan Musial of the St. Louis Cardinals won the National League's Most Valuable Player Award three times, in 1943, 1946 and 1948. He finished second in voting for that award in 1949, 1950, 1951 and 57. From 1943 to 1957, he was in the Top Ten in MVP voting every year but 1945, when he was in the United States Navy serving his country in World War II.

Born Stanley Frank Musial in Donora, Pennsylvania, on November 21, 1920, Stan The Man, as he came to be called, was signed by the Cardinals as an Amateur Free Agent in 1938. Although he was signed as a pitcher, an injury to his shoulder in the Minors ended his pitching career. He made his debut with the Cardinals on September 17, 1941, going 2-4 with two RBI's, against the Boston Braves. He played his entire 22 year career with the Cardinals as an outfielder and occasional first baseman.

The next year, 1942, he became the Cardinals regular left fielder and played in 140 games hitting .315 and driving in 72 runs as the Cards won the National League pennant and beat the Yankees in the World Series.

In 1943, he led the Cards to another World Series, leading the league in hitting with a .357 average, and also led the league in hits with 220, doubles with 48 and triples with 20. In 700 plate appearances that year, amazingly, he struck out just 18 times, once every 39 plate appearances. In his career, he averaged one strikeout for every 18.4 plate appearance. Even the great Ted Williams struck out once in every 13.8 appearances. The Cards lost the Series to the Yankees that year.

In 1944, he hit .347 as the Cardinals won the pennant again and beat the St. Louis Browns in the World Series. He joined the Navy and did not play in 1945 and the Cardinals finished in second place.

He came back in 1946 and hit .365 to lead the league again, pounding out 228 hits, including a league leading 50 doubles and 20 triples. The Cardinals won their fourth pennant in five years, every year except the year Musial was in the service and Musial's first four full years, and beat the Boston Braves in the World Series.

In 1948, he won the batting title with a .376 average and led the league in RBI's with 131. His 39 homers was one less that the 40 hit by Johnny Mize and Ralph Kiner to tie for the league lead and keep Stan from getting the Triple Crown. Even though he was not a big home run hitter, he never led the league in that category and the most he ever hit in one year was his 39 in 1948, he had 475 homers in his career.

The man with the corkscrew batting stance, who wound himself up until he was looking over his right shoulder at the pitcher, looking like he was peeking around a corner at the pitcher, led the National League in hitting seven times. He was named the Most Valuable Player three times, was on every All Star team from 1943-1963 and was Major League Player of the Year twice. He led the National League in on base percentage six times, slugging percentage six times, hits six times, games played five times, doubles eight times, triples five times, runs scored five times and RBI's twice.

His career batting average was .331 and he had 1,951 RBI's and 1,949 runs scored to go with his 475 homers. His career slugging percentage was .559. He hit over .350 four different times and hit over .300 for 16 consecutive years. He hit a record six home runs in All Star Games.

His 725 doubles in the third highest career total ever and his 3,630 hits the fourth highest. Of his 3,630 hits, 1,815 were hit at home and 1,815 on the road according to the Sabre Project. He played almost every day and his total of 3,026 games played is tied for the sixth highest total ever. In a streak that ended in 1957, he played in 895 consecutive games a National League record at the time.

On May 2, 1954, in a doubleheader against the New York Giants at St. Louis, he hit five home runs in the two games, three in the first and two in the second, at the time, the only person to have five home runs in a double header. In 1962, at age 41, he hit .330 with 19 homers and 82 RBI's. Hall of Fame Broadcaster Vin Scully, when asked how good Musial was, once said ' He was good enough to take your breath away.'

He was elected to the Hall of Fame in 1969 in his first year on the ballot with 93 percent of the vote. On his Page at the Hall of Fame, he is quoted as saying 'Unless you give it all you've got, there isn't any sense in playing.'

After his retirement, he stayed active in the Cardinals organization, becoming General Manager in 1967 for just one year, finding that administration was not for him, even though the Cardinals won the pennant that year and beat the Boston Red Sox in the World Series.

A statue of Stan the Man that stood outside the original Busch Stadium, now stands outside the third base gate at the new Busch Stadium. Stan passed away in 2013 but he will always be remembered in St. Louis and all around baseball as one of, if not, the purest hitter of all time.

Darold Knowles of the Oakland Athletics is the only pitcher in history to have pitched in all seven games of a World Series. He did that in 1973 against the New York Mets. Mariano Rivera, of the New York Yankees, holds the record for the most career appearances by a pitcher in the World Series with 24.

ALLIE REYNOLDS' SECOND NO HITTER

At the end of the day on September 27, 1951, the New York Yankees were in first place in the American League. The Yankees, with a record of 93-56, were 2 ½ games ahead of the second place Cleveland Indians who had a 92-60 record. The Yankees had five games to play and the Indians just two.

The Yankees five games left were all with their arch rivals, the third place Boston Red Sox, who were six games out of first and had been mathematically eliminated from the race. However, Boston had an opportunity to keep the Yankees from clinching the pennant if they could win four of the five games or sweep the five.

If the Red Sox could take all five and the Indians won their two, the Indians would win the pennant. If the Sox could take four and the Indians won their two, they would be tied for first with the Yankees. If the Sox swept the Yankees and the Indians won just one of their two, there would be a tie.

In Game 1 of the doubleheader, the Yankees started Allie Reynolds, the Super Chief, against the Red Sox. Reynolds was 16-8 for the season and had pitched a no hitter on July 12 against his old team, the Cleveland Indians, besting the great Bob Feller

1-0. Reynolds was signed by the Indians in 1939 and pitched four years for them, winning 51 and losing 47 with a 3.31 ERA before being traded to the Yankees for Joe Gordon in October of 1946.

The Red Sox sent their left handed Ace Mel Parnell, who was 18-10 for the season, against Reynolds.

Sox center fielder Dom DiMaggio worked a lead off walk in the first inning but second baseman Johnny Pesky grounded into a double play and Reynolds struck out Ted Williams for the last out of the inning.

The Yankees got on the board in the last of the first when short stop Phil Rizzuto and second baseman Jerry Coleman got singles to center to lead off and right fielder Hank Bauer singled to right to score Rizzuto. After third baseman Gil McDougald walked to load the bases, catcher Yogi Berra grounded out and Coleman scored the second run.

In the second, Reynolds struck out right fielder Clyde Vollmer and first baseman Billy Goodman and got short stop Lou Boudreau on a pop out to second. The Yankees went 1-2-3 in the last of the second and Reynolds got the Sox in order in the top of the third.

In the last of the third, Coleman walked and stole second to lead off and, after two were out, McDougald singled to center to score Coleman. Berra then singled to center and McDougald scored when the ball was misplayed in center field and the Yankees were up 4-0.

Reynolds walked Williams with two out in the fourth but got Vollmer to fly to right to end the inning. In the Yankee fourth, first baseman Joe Collins doubled to right, was sacrificed to third by Reynolds and scored the Yankees fifth run on Coleman's sac fly to center.

Reynolds got the Sox in order in the fifth and sixth with two strikeouts in each inning. In the Yankee sixth, left fielder Gene Woodling singled to right and went all the way to third when the ball was misplayed. Collins then homered to make it 7-0.

In the Red Sox seventh, Vollmer walked with two outs but Reynolds got Goodman to ground to third to end the inning. Joe DiMaggio singled for the Yankees with one out in the Yankee seventh but the Sox got out of the inning with no score.

In the Red Sox eighth, Boudreau, Hatfield and Robinson all flied out to right as the Sox went 1-2-3. Woodling led off the Yankee ninth with a homer to make it 8-0 going to the bottom of the ninth with Reynolds still working on a no hitter.

Charley Maxwell pinch hit for reliever Harry Taylor to start the Sox ninth amd grounded to second for the first out. After Dom DiMaggio drew a walk, Johnny Pesky took a called third strike for the second out.

Reynolds was one out away from his second no hitter and the batter at the plate was Ted Williams. Ted was hitting .318 for the year and was probably the last batter in baseball that Reynolds wanted at the plate in that situation.

Ted hit a high pop foul behind the plate and Berra was under it and, unbelievably, dropped the ball. I don't believe that anybody in baseball would have expected Reynolds to get Ted out after that but he got him to hit another pop foul and Yogi caught this one to end the no hitter and guarantee the Yankees at least a tie for first.

In the second game of the doubleheader, the Yankees, behind a complete game by Vic Raschi, got seven runs in the second inning and clinched the pennant with an 11-3 routing of the Sox. It was Raschi's 21st victory of the season.

Reynolds' second no hitter marked the second time in baseball history that a pitcher had thrown two in the same year. Johnny

Vandermeer of the Cincinnati Reds had pitched two in succession in 1938.

The Indians, who did not play on September 28, split their two remaining games with the Tigers to end up five games behind the Yankees in second with the Red Sox 11 games back in third.

The Yankees beat the New York Giants four games to two in the World Series their third World Championship in a row of what would be a streak of five.

Warren Spahn led the league in pitching wins in a single season seven times, the most in baseball history. Pete Alexander was second with seven seasons with the most wins and Bob Feller, Walter Johnson and Tom Glavine were tied for third with five seasons each.

SWEET LOU PINIELLA

One of the reasons I was, and still am, opposed to instant replay in baseball was because it all but eliminated Managers storming the field to argue a call. The average fan who attends a baseball game is there for the entertainment value and what is more entertaining than watching a Manager come screaming out of the dugout, throwing his hat and kicking dirt on the Umpire, fighting for his team.

No one did it better than Sweet Lou Piniella and he got every ounce of energy and drama into every argument. Lou managed baseball the way he played it, as if every strike, out or game was the most important one in the history of the game. Lou played and managed every game like it was for the World Championship. If you look in the dictionary under competitor, you should find a picture of Lou there.

After spending almost eight full years in the Minor Leagues, Lou Piniella played 16 full seasons and part of two others in the Major Leagues and managed in the majors for 23 years.

He was born in Tampa, Florida on August 28, 1943 and attended the University of Tampa before being signed as a Free Agent by the Cleveland Indians in 1962. He was in the minors, working his way from Selma in D ball to Portland in the AAA Pacific Coast League. Along the way, he moved from organization to organization. Starting with his move from Cleveland to Washington in 1964 he then was with Baltimore, Cleveland, again, Seattle and Kansas City.

After he hit .317 with Portland, in 1968, Kansas City gave him his first real chance at the Big Leagues in 1969. He came through with a .282 average and won the Rookie of the Year Award. Lou was an outfielder who made up for what he lacked in natural ability by hard work and giving everything he had every day.

He spent five years in Kansas City, hitting .286, with 45 homers and 348 RBI's. He never was a long ball hitter but always hit for average. On December 7, 1973, Kansas City traded him to the New York Yankees for Lindy McDaniel, a right handed pitcher who would be with the Royals just two years.

Lou spent the rest of his playing career, 11 years, with the Yankees. He hit .295 with 57 homers and 417 RBI's in New York. He played in four World Series with the Yankees, losing to the Cincinnati Reds in 1976 and the Los Angeles Dodgers in 1981 and beating the Dodgers in 1977 and 1978. In 22 World Series games, he batted .319 and had 10 RBI's. In his four World Series, he hit .319 in 22 games.

He made the All Star team in 1972 and hit over .300 seven times. His career batting average was .291 with 102 homers and 766 RBI's. He finished second in batting average in the American League in 1972 and finished fourth two other times.

Lou played his last game on June 16, 1984 and came back to Manage the Yankees in 1986 and 1987 and was replaced by Billy Martin. He came back after Martin was fired in 1988 and finished the year at the helm of the Yankees. He managed the Reds from 1990 to 1992, the Mariners from 1993 to 2002, the Tampa Bay Rays from 2003 to 2005 and the Chicago Cubs from 2007 to 2010.

As a Manager, he only got to one World Series, in 1990, with the Reds, when they swept the Oakland Athletics for the World Championship. His teams made the Post Season in 1990, 1995, 1997, 2001, 2007 and 2008. Except for 1990, when they won it all, his teams lost in the Division Series four times and, got to the LCS in 2001 before losing to the Yankees. Teams he managed won 1,835 games and lost 1,713 and he was named Manager of the Year in the American League in 1995 and 2001 with the Mariners and Manager of the Year in the National League with the Cubs in 2008.

Not counting the short periods he spent with Baltimore in 1964, in which he played in just four games and Cleveland in 1968, playing just six games, Piniella played on or managed teams that won an amazing total of 3,195 games and lost 2,875 games for a grand total of 6,070 games not including post season games.

Lou Piniella was a colorful, effective leader and an astute baseball player and manager. In his 45 plus years as a player and Manager in the Minors and Majors, he was as competitive as anyone who ever played the game. He was born too late but he would have been the ideal Manager of the St. Louis Cardinals old Gas House Gang that won the World Series in 1934.

I know that I am not the only fan that misses the arguments that used to occur regularly before instant replay and wishes that I could see Sweet Lou come storming out of that dugout, throwing his hat and kicking dirt one more time.

SECTION 43

Francisco Rodriguez of the Los Angeles Angels holds the single season pitching record for saves. In 2008, he had 62 saves. Bobby Thigpen, of the Chicago White Sox, has the second most with 57 in 1990 and Eric Gagne of the Los Angeles Dodgers and John Smolz of the Atlanta Braves are tied for third with 55.

THE 1960 WORLD SERIES

The 1960 World Series pitted the American League's New York Yankees against the National League's Pittsburgh Pirates. In 1960, the two leagues still had eight teams each, with no divisions. The winning teams in each league went to the World Series. Each team played 154 games, 22 games against each of the other teams in the league. There was no inter league play as yet.

The Yankees had won the American League pennant with a 97-57 record, beating out the second place Baltimore Orioles by eight games. The Pirates were 95-59 and had beaten the second place Milwaukee Braves by seven games.

Both teams had their league's Most Valuable Player on their roster. Short stop Dick Groat of the Pirates had won the National League award with a .325 batting average. Yankee Right fielder Roger Maris won it in the American League with a .283 average, 40 homers and 112 RBI's.

It was Maris' first of two consecutive MVP awards. In 1961 when he broke Babe Ruth's record with 61 homers, he also had 141 RBI's. Coincidentally, 1961 was the year the American League schedule expanded to 162 games, due to the addition of the Minnesota Twins and Los Angeles Angels, causing baseball to add an asterisk to Maris' record because it was achieved in eight more games than the Babe's.

Pirate pitcher Vern Law, with a record of 20-9 and an ERA of 3.08 had won the Cy Young award. There was only one Cy Young Award given for all of baseball until 1967, when they began to award one to the top pitcher in each league.

Law was on the mound to start Game 1 against Yankee Art Ditmar. The Yankees scored first when Maris homered to right to make it 1-0. The Pirates came right back with three in the last of the first, driving out Ditmar after he had gotten only one out. Center fielder Bill Virdon walked and stole second and scored on a double by Groat. Left fielder Bob Skinner then singled to center to score Groat, stole second and scored on a single by right fielder Roberto Clemente, to make it 3-1.

The Yankees got one back in the fourth when first baseman Moose Skowron singled to drive in Maris and make it 3-2. Mazeroski homered with third baseman Don Haok aboard in the fourth to make it 5-2 and the Pirates made it 6-2 with one in the sixth.

That was all the scoring until Yankee third baseman Gil McDougald singled and pinch hitter Elston Howard homered in the ninth to make the final 6-4. Law, who went seven innings, giving up just two runs, got the win.

The Yankees came back to win Game 2, 16-3, pounding out 19 hits, including two home runs and five RBI's by center fielder Mickey Mantle, to tie the Series at 1-1 going to New York for Game 3. Yankee starter Bob Turley got the win.

The Yankees continued to hit the ball in Game 3, winning 10-0, after getting six in the first inning. Mantle had his third homer in two days and second baseman Bobby Richardson had a grand slam in the first. Whitey Ford pitched a complete game four hitter for the win.

Law started for Pittsburgh and Ralph Terry for New York, in Game 4. The game was scoreless until the last of the fourth when Skowron homered to put the Yankees up, 1-0.
First baseman Gino Cimoli led off the fifth for the Pirates and singled. Catcher Smokey Burgess then reached on a fielder's choice. Pitcher Law then doubled to score Cimoli and Virdon singled to score Burgess and Law with the tying and go ahead runs.

In the Yankee seventh, Skowron doubled, McDougald singled and Skowron scored when Richardson grounded to second to make it 3-2 and that was the final. Law got his second win of the Series and the run he scored turned out to be the winning run.

In Game 5, the Pirates knocked Ditmar out in the second inning, getting three runs with the big hit a two run double by Mazeroski, to lead 3-0. In the Yankee second Howard doubled, went to third on a ground out and scored on Kubek's grounder to first to make it 3-1. In the third Groat led off with a double and Clemente drove him in with a single to make it 4-1. Maris homered for the Yankees in the third to make it 4-2 and the Pirates added one in the ninth and won, 5-2. Haddix got the win for the Pirates and they led three games to one going back to Pittsburgh.

Facing elimination, the Yankees teed off on Friend and five other Pirate pitchers, scoring 12 runs on 17 hits including three each by Yogi Berra, playing left field, Maris and John Blanchard, the catcher, to win 12-0. Ford pitched another complete game shut out, giving up just seven hits for his second win of the Series to force a Game 7.

Law started Game 7 for the Pirates against Bullet Bob Turley for the Yankees. Turley gave up a two run homer to first baseman Rocky Nelson in the first and was removed after giving up a lead off single in the second. The Pirates got two more in the second after Turley was gone and it was 4-0.

Skowron homered for the Yankees in the fifth to make it 4-1. The Yankees got four in the sixth to go up 5-4 when Mantle drove in one and Berra hit a three run homer. The Yankees got two more in the top of the eighth to make it 7-4. In the bottom of the eighth, the Pirates came back for five as Groat and Clemente singled in runs and Hal Smith, who came in the game to catch in the top of the eighth, after the Pirates had a pinch runner for Burgess, hit a three run homer to make it 9-7.

The Yankees stunned the Pittsburgh crowd by coming back to tie the game against Friend and Haddix in the top of the ninth with an RBI single by Mantle, scoring Richardson, and Yogi Berra's RBI ground out scoring McDougald.

In the top of the ninth, with Bob Terry, who had come in to get the last out in the eighth inning, on the mound for the Yankees, Mazeroski led off the inning. With the count 1-0, Mazeroski hit a long fly ball into the seats in left field for the only walk off home run in the seventh game of a World Series in baseball history and the Pirates were World Champions.

Despite Mazeroski's dramatic home run and his eight hits, five RBI's and four runs scored, Bobby Richardson, of the Yankees, with 11 hits in 30 at bats, eight runs scored and 12 RBI's was the Series MVP. Mazeroski was voted into the Hall of Fame by the Veteran's Committee in 2001.

SECTION 44

Raphael Palmeiro holds the record for the most games played with no World Series appearances with 2,831 games. Ken Griffey, Jr., is second with 2,671, Andre Dawson, third at 2,627 and Ernie Banks fourth at 2,528. Of the four, three are Hall of Fame members. Palmeiro is the only one that isn't in the Hall.

TONY GWYNN

Anthony Keith Gwynn, Sr., was born in Los Angeles, California, on May 9, 1960. After high school, he attended San Diego State University, where he was an All Western Athletic Conference selection in both basketball and baseball. He was drafted by the San Diego Clippers basketball team of the National Basketball Association in the 10th round of the 1981 draft and also by the San Diego Padres in the third round of the draft that same year.

He opted for baseball and signed with the Padres on June 16. That year, between AA Walla Walla, Washington, in the Northwest League League and Amarillo, Texas in the AA Texas League, he hit .375 in 65 games with 16 homers and 56 RBI's. He spent the first part of the next year at Hawaii in the AAA Pacific Coast League, hitting .328 before making his Major League debut with the Padres on July 19, 1982. Against the Phillies that first game, he got two hits in four at bats and drove in a run.

He played in 54 games at the end of that season, hitting .289. In 1983, his first full season, he played in 86 games, hitting .309, the lowest average he would post in 19 full seasons in the Majors. In his second full year, he came into his own, winning the batting title with a .351 average and leading the league in hits with 213.

Opposition teams quickly found that Gwynn hit well to all fields and Tommy Lasorda, legendary Dodgers Manager, is quoted on Gwynn's page at the Hall of Fame as saying that year 'How do you defend against a hitter who hits the ball down the left field line, down the right field line and up the middle?'

He also made the All Star team that year for the first of 15 times. The Padres won the National League Western Division that year with a 92-70 record. They beat the Chicago Cubs in the League Championship Series but lost to the Detroit Tigers in the World Series, in five games. Also on that Padres team were first baseman Steve Garvey and Closer Rich 'Goose' Gossage. Gwynn hit just .263, going 5-19 in the Series.

He would win the batting title a total of eight times, tying him with the great Honus Wagner for the most times in National League history. He won the title in 1984, 1986, 1987, 1988 and 1999. and then, from 1994 to 1997, in succession. In the five year period from 1993 to 1997, he got 916 hits in 2,545 at bats for an amazing five year average of .360. In the 1994 season, shortened by the players' strike, he hit .394 and hit over .350 six times in his career.

In 1998, the Padres won the West again with a 98-64 record, beat the Houston Astros in four games in the NLDS and the Atlanta Braves, four games to two in the NLCS and were swept in the World Series by the New York Yankees. This was Gwynn's last World Series and he hit .500 with eight hits in 16 at bats in losing cause.

The Padres had made the Playoffs in 1996 but were swept by the St. Louis Cardinals in the NLDS. He was in two NLDS, two ALCS and two World Series in his career and hit .306 in 27 games and 108 at bats.

He spent his entire 20 year career with the Padres, in the area where he grew up, and was always referred to as Mr. Padre. He had 3,141 hits in his career, 19th best of all time, and a .338

lifetime batting average, tied for 18th best, in 9,288 at bats. In addition to his other records mentioned above, he led the league in hits seven times, in singles seven times and won five Gold Gloves and seven Silver Sluggers. Perhaps the best measurement of his ability as a hitter was the fact that, in every full year of his career except his first full year, 1983, he had more walks than strikeoouts and led the league in the least strikeouts per at bat 10 times.

He won the Branch Rickey Award for exceptional community service, in 1995, the Lou Gehrig Award, given to the player who best exhibits the character of Lou Gehrig, in 1998, and the Roberto Clemente Award, given for a combination of good play and community work, in 1999.

He was voted into the Baseball Hall of Fame in 2007 with 532 of 545 votes. He passed away on June 16, 2014, shortly after his 54th birthday after a battle with cancer.

His son, Tony, Jr., had an eight year Major League career, two of the years with the Padres, as an outfielder, with a career batting average of .283. He has recently taken a position with the Los Angeles Dodgers as a broadcaster on their Post Game Show.

His younger brother, Chris, played ten years as a Major League outfielder, with the Dodgers, Kansas City Royals and Padres, with a .261 batting average.

SECTION 45

Before the first recognized World Series in 1903, there were several held that are considered exhibitions today, In 1885, the Providence Grays swept the New York Metropolitans in three games. Old Hoss Radbourn pitched and won all three games for Providence, giving up just three runs in three complete games. He had won 59 and lost 12 in the regular season that year with a 1.38 ERA in 679 innings.

THE MIRACLE METS

In their first year of existence, 1962, the New York Mets lost 120 games, the most losses in a season in baseball history. In their first six years, under Managers Casey Stengel and Wes Westrum, they lost an average of 108 games per year. In 1968, former Dodger great Gil Hodges was hired to take over as Manager. He had been managing the Washington Senators but the Mets traded for him.

In 1968, under Hodges, the Mets won 73 and lost 89 and finished in ninth place. They went into the 1969 season with not much higher expectations even though they had just had the best year in franchise history.

In the first month of the season, they won 9 and lost 11. They managed to lose 12 of their next 21 and, on May 27th, they were in fourth place, nine games behind the Cubs with a record of 18-23.

From May 28 until June 10, they won 11 in a row, moving into second place but still trailing the Cubs by seven games. They won 49 and lost 33 from then until September 5. On that day, the Mets were in second place, but still 4 ½ games behind the Cubs with a record of 78-57.

They won their next ten games in a row and moved into first place, 3 ½ games ahead of the Cubs. From September 5th until the end of the season they won 22 and lost just five games, including another nine game winning streak, from September 21 until October 1.
On September 12, they won a double header against the Pittsburgh Pirates in Pittsburgh. In Game 1, Koosman, the starting pitcher, pitched a complete game shut out and singled in the fifth to drive in the only run of the game as they won 1-0. In Game 2, Cardwell, the starting pitcher, pitched eight innings of shut out ball and singled in the second to drive in the only run of the game and they won again, 1-0. The Mets could always find way to win as they went down the stretch.

They ended up the Division Winner, eight games ahead of the Cubs who lost 18 of 26 in that same time period.

They had won with pitching and defense. Seaver had won his last ten decisions to finish 25-7 for the year and Koosman had won his last five to finish 17-9. Nolan Ryan was bothered by a groin injury all season and was 6-3. The bullpen with Closer Ron Taylor at 9-3, with a 2.72 ERA in 59 games, Tug McGraw 9-3 and 2.24 in 42 games and Cal Koonce at 6-3, 4.99 in 40 games did their share.

They certainly didn't hit. Their team batting average of .242 was seventh in the league, they scored 598 runs, ninth in the league and hit only 109 homers, eighth. Left fielder Cleon Jones at .340 and right fielder Art Shamsky were the only regulars at or above .300.

They played the Atlanta Braves in the National League Championship Series. The Braves, with a 93-69 record, had won the Eastern Division by three games over the San Francisco Giants.

In Game 1, at Atlanta, the Mets started Seaver against the Braves Phil Neikro. The Mets scored first, getting two in the second when right fielder Art Shamsky singled, second baseman Ken Boswell walked and catcher Jerry Grote singled in Shamsky with Boswell going to third. Boswell scored on a passed ball and it was 2-0, Mets. The Braves came back with one in the last of the second with a double by left fielder Rico Carty, who moved to third when right fielder Orlando Cepeda reached on an error and scored on a sac fly to left by third baseman Clete Boyer.

In the Braves third, second baseman Felix Millan, center fielder Tony Gonzalez and right fielder Hank Aaron hit consecutive doubles to make it 3-2. The Mets came back in the fourth when, with two out, first baseman Ed Kranepool singled, Grote walked and short stop Ken Harrelson drove them both in with a triple to right, to make it 4-3 Mets. The Braves regained the lead on solo homers by Gonzalez in the fifth and Aaron in the seventh.

It was 5-4 Braves, going to the eighth. Third baseman Wayne Garrett doubled to left and left fielder Cleon Jones singled to score him and tie the score. Shamsky then singled to right and Kranepool grounded to first but the throw home went wild and Jones scored and Shamsky and Kranepool ended up at second and third. Harrelson was intentionally walked to load the bases and J. C. Martin, batting for Seaver, singled to right to score both runners and the score was 9-5.

Taylor came in in relief of Seaver and shut out the Braves in the eighth and ninth and the Mets were up 1-0 in the series. Seaver got the win, going seven innings and giving up five runs on eight hits.

In Game 2, the Mets pounded out thirteen hits and easily went up 2-0 in the series, winning 11-6. Koosman started for the Mets but lasted only 4 2/3 innings and gave up six runs on seven hits. Taylor and McGraw finished the game and held the Braves scoreless, with Taylor getting the win. The Mets scored in every inning but the sixth, eighth and ninth, getting two run homers from Agee, Boswell and Jones. The Mets were going home for Game 3, needing just one win to go to the World Series.

In Game 3, the Braves got off to a 2-1 lead against the Mets Gary Gentry when Aaron hit a two run homer in the first. In the Braves third, Gentry gave up a single to Gonzalez and a double to Aaron to lead off the inning but Nolan Ryan came in in relief and shut down the

Braves with no runs getting two strikeouts.

In the Mets third, Agee hit a solo homer and Boswell got a two run homer in the fourth to make it 3-2 Mets. In the Braves fifth they regained the lead when Cepeda hit a two run homer to make it 4-3. Ryan led off the Mets fifth with a single to right and Garrett homered to make it 5-4 Mets. Jones then doubled to right and scored on a Boswell homer to make it 6-4.

With two out in the Mets sixth Grote doubled and, with two out, Agee singled to left to score him and that was the final, Mets 7 Braves 4 and the Mets were in the World Series. The Baltimore Orioles, who were 109-53 on the season and won the American League East by 19 games and swept the Minnesota Twins would be their opponent.

The Mets started their Ace Tom Seaver, National League Cy Young Award winner, with a 25-7 record, in Game 1 against the Orioles Mike Cuellar, the American League Cy Young Award winner, who was 23-11 during the season and shared the Award with Detroit's Denny McLain who was 24-9.

The Orioles got first blood in the last of the first when left fielder Don Buford hit a lead off homer to right field to make it 1-0. They got three more in the fourth when, with two out catcher Elrod Hendricks singled, second baseman Davey Johnson walked and shortstop Mark Belanger singled to score Hendricks. Cuellar then singled to drive in Johnson and help his own cause. Buford doubled to right, scoring Belanger and it was 4-0

O's. The Mets would get a single run in the seventh but that was the scoring as Cuellar pitched a complete game six hitter, with eight strikeouts, to get the win. Seaver went just five innings giving up all four runs on six hits and got the loss.

In Game 2, the Mets Koosman and Orioles Dave McNally hooked up in a pitchers' duel. The Mets got a homer from Donn Clendenon to lead off the fourth and the O's got it back in the seventh when Blair singled, stole second with two out and scored on third baseman Brooks Robinsons' single to,left to tie it at 1-1.

It stayed at 1-1 unto the top of the ninth when, with two outs, third baseman Ed Charles and Jerry Grote both singled to left and Weis singled to drive in the go ahead and eventual winning run. In the Baltimore ninth, Koosman got Buford on a fly to right and Blair on a grounder to shoirt and the O's were down to their last out. Koosman then walked Frank R obinson and Boog Powell to put the tying run on second. Taylor relieved Koosmand and he got Brooks Robinson to ground to third and the Mets had tied the Series at 1-1.

In Game 3, Gary Gentry and Nolan Ryan teamed up to shut out the Orioles on four hits while the Mets were getting five off Jim Palmer and Dave Leonhard to win 5-0. Agee led off the first with a homer and Gentry doubled in the second to drive in two and give himself a 3-0 lead. The Mets got another in the sixth when Grote doubled to score Boswell who was on with a single and added another in the eighth on a solo homer by Kranepool. The Mets led 2-1 going to Game 4.

Game 4 matched Seaver and Cuellar again and it was a pitchers' duel. The Mets scored first in the second when Clendenon hit his second led off homer of the Series. It stayed 1-0 until the top of the ninth when Seaver gave up singles to Frank Robinson and Powell putting runners on first and third. Brooks Robinson then hit a sacrifice fly to score the tying run.

The Mets didn't score in the last of the ninth and Seaver kept the O's scoreless in the top of the tenth. In the bottom of the ninth, Dick Hall came in in relief for the Orioles and gave up a double to Grote. Weis was intentionally walked and Rod Gaspar came in to run for Grote. Pete Richert came in to relieve Hall and Martin, pinch hitting for Seaver, bunted to sacrifice the runners up and Richert threw wild to first allowing Gaspar to score the winning run and the Mets were up 3-1 with an elimination game coming up at home.

The Mets started Koosman in Game 5 against the Orioles McNally again, in a rematch of Game 2. The Orioles got three in the second to take the lead when Mark Belanger singled to right and McNally helped his own cause with a homer to make it 2-0. Frank Robinson then hit a solo homer to make it 3-0 after three.

The Mets got two back in the sixth when Clendenon got his third homer of the Series with Jones on base. In the seventh, Weis tied the score with a homer to left and it was 3-3 going to the eighth. With Eddie Watt in in relief of McNally, in the bottom of the eighth, Jones led off with a double and right fielder Ron Swoboda doubled to left to drive in Jones with the go ahead run. When Grote reached on an error by first baseman Boog Powell, Swoboda scored to make it 5-3.

Koosman, who had shut out the Orioles since giving up the three runs in the second, got the O's with no runs in the ninth and the Mets were the unlikely World Champs. Koosman got the win, his second of the Series pitching a complete game.

Donn Clendenon, who was named Series MVP, was 5-14 with three homers, four RBI's and four runs scored in the five games. Koosman, won two games and pitched 17 2/3 innings with a 2.04 ERA.

The next two years, the Mets would finish in third place, with identical 83-79 records, but they had successfully completed their Miracle Year.

SECTION 46

Gene Conley was the first Major League baseball player ever to win World Championships in two different sports. He did it, as a pitcher, with the Milwaukee Braves, of baseball, in 1957, and, as a forward, with the Boston Celtics in the National Basketball Association from 1959-1961.

BOB FELLER

On August 23, 1936, Bob Feller made his first Major League start as a pitcher with the Cleveland Indians. He faced the St. Louis Browns in Cleveland's League Park # 2 and pitched a complete game six hitter, giving up just one run in the sixth inning as the Indians won, 4-1. Feller struck out 15 Browns' batters that day, getting every batter in the Browns starting lineup, except third baseman Harlond Clift, at least once.

On August 30, he made his second start and lasted just five innings, giving up four runs on six hits to the Red Sox in Boston as the Indians lost, 5-1, and he got the loss. He got his second loss on September 3, when he only lasted one inning, giving up five runs on three hits and three walks, against the Yankees in New York.

Four days later, he got his second win, again pitching a complete game, again against the Browns, this time giving up seven hits and one run and striking out ten against the Browns. Six days later, he struck out 17 Philadelphia Athletics batters, while pitching another complete game, giving up two runs on two hits.

He ended the 1936 season with five wins and three losses, throwing 62 innings and striking out 76, with eight starts and five complete games. Not a spectacular beginning but not bad for a seventeen year old.

That's right, at age 17, three months and two weeks before his eighteenth birthday, Bob Feller was already making a name for himself as a strikeout pitcher. Major League batters were already finding out what Hall of Famer Ted Lyons said later ' It wasn't until you hit against him that you knew how fast he really was, until you saw with your own eyes that ball jumping at you.'

Robert William Andrew Feller was born November 3, 1918, in Van Meter, Iowa. He was signed as a Free Agent by the Indians at age 17.

In 1937, at age 18, he won nine and lost seven, with a 3.39 ERA. In 1938, he began, at age 19, to come into his own, winning 17 and losing 11 and leading the league in strike outs with 240.

In 1939, he won 24 and lost 9 with a 2.85 ERA and 246 strikeouts. In 1940, with 27 wins, 11 losses, a 2.61 ERA and 261 strikeouts, he won the Triple Crown for pitching and was named the Major League Player of the Year. On April 16 of that year, he threw his first of three no hitters, beating the Chicago White Sox, 1-0.

In 1941, he won 25 and lost 13, led the league in strikeouts with 260 and had a 3.15 ERA. In that period, from 1939 to 1941, he won 76 and lost just 33 while striking out 767 batters.

On December 9, 1941, the day after Pearl Harbor, he enlisted in the Navy, even though he had a deferment, and was the first of many Major League players to do so. He was in the Navy from then until late in the 1945 season, missing almost four full seasons at the prime of his career.

He returned to the Indians on August 24, 1945, nine years and one day after he made his first Major League start. He started nine games at the end of that year, won five and lost three and had six complete games.

In 1946, he came back like he'd never been away, winning a league leading, 26, and losing 15 with a 2.18 ERA and 348 strikeouts, a modern record total, which stood until Sandy Koufax struck out 382 in 1965. He also had his second no hitter on April 30, beating the New York Yankees 1-0. He also had 36 complete games to lead the league.

In 1947, he led the league in wins again with 20 wins and 11 losses and a 2.68 ERA and 196 strike outs. It was his sixth season with 20 or more wins and he he also threw his third no hitter on July 1, beating the Tigers 2-1.

In the five full seasons, before and after his service time, he had won 121 and lost just 59 while striking out 1,311 batters, an average of 24 wins and 262 strikeouts per year. If he had been able to pitch those four years, at the peak of his career, it is not unreasonable to assume that he would have at least had four average years. If he did, he would have finished with 357 wins, tenth highest of all time, and 3,670 strikeouts, sixth highest of all time.

In 1948, when the Indians won their only pennant while he was with them, he won 19 and lost 15 with a 3.56 ERA. In the World Series, against the Boston Braves, which the Indians won four games to two, he lost the two games his team lost. In Game 1, with Johnny Sain pitching a four hitter for the Braves, Feller gave up just one run on two hits to lose, 1-0. The run scored in the eighth with two outs when Braves right fielder Tommy Holmes hit a little bloop pop fly down the right field line to drive in the only run of the game. In Game 5 he gave up seven runs in 6 1/3 innings as the Indians lost 11-5.

In 1951, at the ripe old age of 32, fifteen years after his debut, he had his sixth season with 20 or more wins, winning a league high 22 and losing just eight with a 3.50 ERA. He also had his third no hitter on July 1, beating the Detroit Tigers, 2-1.

He spent his entire career with the Indians, winning a total of 266 games while losing 162 and compiling a 3.25 ERA. He made 484 starts and threw 279 complete games with 2,581 strikeouts. He was elected to the Hall of Fame in 1962 and made the All Star team eight times.

In 2013, the Bob Feller Act of Valor Award was created by MLB and the Navy to honor baseball players and Navy personnel who reflect the values of honor, courage and commitment in recognition of Feller's dedication to his country. Feller received six campaign ribbons and eight battle stars during his almost four years service.

On his page at the Hall of Fame, he is quoted as saying about his service ' I didn't worry about losing my baseball career. We needed to win the war. I wanted to do my part.'

Ty Cobb won more league batting titles, with 11, than any other player in baseball history. Honus Wagner and Tony Gwynn were tied for second with eight and Rogers Hornsby, Rod Carew and Stan Musial had seven each. Ted Williams was next with six.

AMERICAN LEAGUE FINISH, 1949

The 1949 New York Yankees led the American League race from Opening Day until September 26th when they fell into second place behind the Boston Red Sox after being swept by the Sox in a three game series in Boston. With five games to play the Red Sox took over first and led the Yankees by one game.

The Red Sox traveled to Washington for a three game series with the Senators and the Yankees went home to play three against the Philadelphia Athletics. Both the Yankees and the Red Sox won two of those three games and the stage was set for a dramatic two game series in New York with the Red Sox coming in.

The Sox needed to win just one of the two games to clinch the pennant while the Yankees would have to sweep the series to win the pennant. With the Sox ahead by one with two games left there would be a winner here, with no possible tie and playoff.

The teams had been evenly matched during the season, with the Yankees winning 11 times and the Sox nine. The Sox had scored a total of 102 runs in their meetings and the Yankees 101.

One of the highlights of the American League Season that year had been a series between the two in Boston June 28, 29 and 30.

The Yankees came into Boston, leading the second place Cleveland Indians by three games and the third place Red Sox by seven. The Yankees had been without their Star center fielder Joe DiMaggio, all year. DiMaggio, who had won the MVP in 1947, for the third time, and had hit .320 and led the league in homers with 39 and RBI's with 155 in 1948, hadn't played all year due to a bone spur on his heel.

With much publicity, Joe returned to the lineup for the series with the hated Red Sox hoping to put the Red Sox out of contention. In Game 1, which the Yankees, won 5-4, the Yankee Clipper singled and scored one run and had a two run homer, driving in Phil Rizzuto, putting the Yankees up 5-0 and they would hold on to win. In Game 2, he hit two homers, one a three run shot and the other a solo in the eighth that put the Yankees ahead to stay, 8-7. In Game 3, he hit a three run homer off Boston Ace Mel Parnell in the seventh to give the a four run lead. In the three games, he went 5-11, with four homers, nis didn't know it at the time, but the Sox would be back.uts and, in his career,

On October 1st, the Sox started Parnell, 25-7, 2.77 ERA and 27 complete games, against Allie Reynolds, 17-6, for the Yankees. In the first, Vern Stephens hit a sac fly to put the Sox up 1-0. In the third, Reynolds walked Johnny Pesky, Ted Williams and Stephens to load the bases. Doerr singled to left, scoring Pesky and Joe Page came in to relieve Reynolds with the bases loaded. He walked the first two batters to force in two runs and make it 4-0, Boston, before getting the last two outs on strikeouts.

The Yankees got two in the fourth when DiMaggio hit a ground rule double and scored on Henrich's single to right. Lindell then singled Henrich to third and he scored on Coleman's sac fly. In the fourth Rizzuto and Henrich singled to put two on and Berra singled to center to score Rizzuto and, after DiMaggio loaded the bases with an infield hit, Billy Johnson hit into a double play, scoring Henrich with the tying run. Johnny Lindell homered in the eighth and the Yankees had won 5-4. Joe Page, who relieved Reynolds in the third and shut out the Sox the rest of the way, got the win, his 13th of the year.ne RBI's and five runs scored after not having batted all season.

The Yankees started Vic Raschi, 20-10 against Ellis Kinder, 23-5 in the game for all the marbles. In a classic pitchers' duel the Yankees went into the bottom of the eighth leading 1-0. Tommy Henrich led off the Yankee eighth with a solo homer and, after two out, Johnny Lindell, Hank Bauer and Billy Johnson singled to load the bases and Gerry Coleman hit a bases clearing double to make it 5-0, Yankees.

In the ninth, with one out, 1949 MVP winner, Ted Williams walked and Stephens singled to center. Doerr then tripled to deep center to score them and, after Al Zarrilla flied to short center, Goodman singled to center to score Doerr and make it 5-4. With the tying run on base and the potential winning run at the plate, Raschi then got Birdie Tebbetts to foul out to first and the Yankees had come back to win the pennant.

The Yankees would go on to beat the Dodgers in the Series four games to one, the first of five consecutive Yankee World Series wins.

After having been in first place or tied for first place all year, except for three days, the Yankees had come close to blowing the pennant but held on through one of the most exciting finishes in American League history.

Octavio Dotel, a right handed pitcher, from the Dominican Republic played for more different franchises in Major League Baseball than anyone in history. From 199 to 2013, he played for 13 franchises, seven in the National League, the Mets, Astros, Braves, Pirates, Dodgers, Rockies and Cardinals. He played for six American League franchises, the Athletics, Yankees, Royals, White Sox, Blue Jays and Tigers.

ICHIRO SUZUKI

According to Baseball Reference, there are 1,349 players who played Major League Baseball in 2015. Of these players, 978 were born in the United States and 391 were born in other countries. Of the total, 10 were born in Japan.

One of those, Ichiro Suzuki was the first Japanese born position player to play in the Major Leagues. Of all the foreign born players, he may have had more of an impact on the game than any other.

Before coming to America, Ichiro played for the Orix Blue Wave in the Japanese Pacific League from 1992 until 2000. He averaged .353 in Japan with 1,278 hits in those nine years. He was named to the All Star Team seven times, won the League Most Valuable Player Award three times, led the league in hitting seven times, in hits five times and in on base percentage five times.

He came to America to play for the Seattle Mariners and made his debut on April 2, 2001, at age 27. All he did that first year, in a strange country, was bat .350, lead the league in hits with 242 and stolen bases with 56. He won the Rookie of the Year and Most Valuable Player Awards in the American League and led his team to a 116 win season to top the Western Division. They beat the Cleveland Indians in the American League Division Series but lost to the Yankees in the League Championship series.

Over his first ten years, he won the American League batting title seven times, hit over .300, with over 200 hits, made the All Star Team and won the Gold Glove every year. From 2001 until 2012, he played in 157 or more games every year except one, 2009, when he played in 'only' 146.

He spent 12 years in Seattle and averaged 211 hits per season, with a batting average of .322 and also averaged 36.5 stolen bases per year.

Ichiro achieved almost Folk Hero status in Seattle. The first time I saw him play in Safeco Field, in 2004, the fans were giving him standing ovations for making routine plays in the field. At that time, one of the local television stations had a three story picture of him on the side of its building. He is an exceptionally talented fielder with a strong and accurate arm with a great sense of where he is on the field. In addition to his hitting and fielding, he is a gifted base runner with great base stealing ability.

In 2012, he became a Free Agent and signed with the New York Yankees. He spent three years with the Yankees, batting .281 and amassing another 311 hits. In 2012, the Yankees won the American League East and went to the Playoffs, beating the Baltimore Orioles in the ALDS and Ichiro went 5-23 for a .217 average and, in the ALCS, which the Yankees lost to the Detroit Tigers, he was 6-17 for a .353 average.

After the 2014 season he became a Free Agent again and signed with the Miami Marlins where he hit only .229 with 91 hits, playing in 153 games but often as a defensive replacement late in games. As of the end of the 2015 season, he has played in 2,357 games without appearing in a World Series which puts him 13th the on the all time list for this dubious honor. Rafael Palmeiro has the record for the most games played without a Series appearance at 2,831.

Ichiro is one of the hardest working players in the game when it comes to conditioning. His work ethic has made it possible for him to stay healthy and continue to play as many games as he has in a season. Amazingly, from 2010 through 2012, when he was 37-39 years old, he missed only one game of 486 his team played.

His unique batting style where he seems to reach back to hit the ball after already starting towards first base earns him more than his share of infield hits. He has slowed down somewhat and appears that, even he may eventually come to the end of his career.

At the end of 2015, his career batting average in his 16 years in MLB was .314, he had 2,935 hits, 1,348 runs and 498 stolen bases. That for a career that started in this country at age 27. One can only imagine what his numbers would be like if he had come to America in 1992 instead of spending nine years in Japan.

In his 25 year career, between Japan and the United States, he has a total of 4,213 hits. There are those who argue that his years in Japan should not be considered in evaluating his career because the quality of the competition there is not as high as in MLB. No matter how you feel about that, you have to marvel at Ichiro's accomplishments.

He is a member of the Miami Marlins as we enter the 2016 season. He lacks just 65 hits to reach the 3,000 hit mark in MLB, which is generally considered to be a mark that will guarantee Hall of Fame recognition. Whether he makes it or not, and I am confident he will, this amazing athlete, competitor and representative of his native country has made a great impression on American baseball.

SECTION 49

Mariano Rivera, of the New York Yankees, holds the record for most games pitched in postseason play with 96 games and also for the most saves, 42. Jeff Nelson is second in games pitched with 55, with the Yankees and Seattle Mariners. Brad Lidge, who pitched in postseason for the Houston Astros and the Philadelphia Phillies, is second in saves with 18.

LOU GEHRIG

Wally Pipp, who started the 1925 season as the New York Yankee first baseman, is quoted on Lou Gehrig's page in the Hall of Fame as saying, ' I took the two most expensive aspirin in history'. On June 1, 1925, Pipp kept himself out of the Yankee game because he had a headache. The man who took his place that day, Lou Gehrig, played first base in every game the Yankees played from that date until he took himself out of a game with an illness on May 2, 1939, 2,130 games later.

Louis Henry Gehrig was born in New York on June 19, 1903 and attended Commerce High School and Columbia University in New York. According to the Sabre Project, when he was 17 years old, his Commerce High School team played a game against Lane Tech High School in Chicago in Cub's Park, later Wrigley Field in Chicago. The game, sponsored by the City of Chicago, went to the ninth inning with Commerce up 8-6 when Gehrig hit a grand slam out of the Park to bring him to national attention.

The Sabre Project biography says that, after high school he went to Columbia on a football scholarship but played baseball his sophomore year. That year, he hit .444 with a .937 slugging average and seven homers in 19 games and he was signed as a Free Agent by the Yankees.

He spent most of the next two years at Hartford in the Eastern League where he hit .304 and .369. He made his debut with the Yankees on June 15, 1923 but only played 13 games with them that year, hitting .423 with 11 hits in 26 at bats. In 1924, he played in just 10 games with the Yankees and hit .500, with six hits in 12 at bats.

In 1925, his first full year in the Majors, he hit just .295 but would improve to .313 in 1926 and helped the Yankees won the pennant but they then lost the World Series to the St. Louis Cardinals. In the first of seven Series he would play in, and the only one as a loser, he hit .341. He hit .373 with 47 homers and 173 RBI's in 1927 and was named American League MVP. The Yankees won the pennant again and beat the Pittsburgh Pirates in the World Series. He hit .308 in that Series.

In 1928, he hit .374 and had 27 homers and 147 RBI's and the Yankees went to the Series for the third straight year, beating the Cardinals in four straight. In four games he hit .545 going 6-11 with four home runs and nine RBI's. In 1931, he hit .341 and led the league in homers with 46 and RBI's with 185, the highest RBI total in American League history, a record which still stands.

In 1932, he hit .349 and the Yankees won another World Series, beating the Chicago Cubs in four games and Gehrig hit .529 going 9-17 with three homers and eight RBI's in the Series.

He won the Triple Crown in 1934, with a .363 batting average, 49 homers and 166 RBI's. From 1926 until 1937, he would hit over .300 every year.

In 1936, he was Most Valuable Player again, hitting .354 and driving in 152 runs. The Yankees won the pennant and beat the New York Giants in the World Series. Gehrig hit .292 with two homers and six RBI's in the Series.

In 1937, he hit .351 in the regular season and .294 in the Series as the Yankees beat the New York Giants. In 1938, his average fell to .295 but the Yankees won the pennant again and Lou hit just .286 in his last World Series.

On May 2, 1939, suffering the effects of the disease that would kill him two years later, amyotropic lateral sclerosis, or ALS, later known as Lou Gehrig's Disease, he took himself out of the starting lineup for the first time in 2,130 games.

On July 4, 1939, with everyone aware that Lou was dying from the disease, Lou Gehrig Appreciation Day was held at Yankee Stadium. Lou addressed the crowd that day and made the famous speech where he declared ' Today I consider myself the luckiest man on the face of the earth'. He passed away from the effects of the disease on June 2, 1941, shortly before his 38th birthday.

In his relatively short career, he only played 15 full seasons, Lou Gehrig had one of the most productive careers in baseball history. His consecutive game streak of 2,130, was broken by Cal Ripken but is still, and probably always will be, the second longest streak in baseball history. During that streak he acquired the nickname the Iron Horse.

Baseball player's uniform numbers were assigned according to where they usually batted in the lineup in those days and Gehrig wore the number 4 because he batted fourth, or cleanup, behind the greatest number 3 in the history of the game, Babe Ruth.

He played in seven World Series, six of which the Yankees won. In the seven World Series he played in, the Yankees won 28 games and lost just six, sweeping four games, four times. He won two Most Valuable Player Awards, in 1927 and 1936, won the Triple Crown in 1934 and played in every All Star Game from its inception in 1933 until 1939. He hit more Grand Slam Home Runs than anyone in baseball history, 23 and his record of 185 RBI's in a single season may never be equaled.

He won the batting title once, the home run title three times, led the league in RBI's five times, in on base percentage five times, in runs scored four times, in total bases four times and in doubles twice. In his seven World Series, he averaged .361 with 10 homer and 35 RBI's and a .731 slugging percentage in 34 games.

His career batting average of .340 is the 17th highest of all time, his .447 on base percentage fifth highest and his slugging percentage of .632 the third highest. He hit 493 homers and his 1,995 RBI's is the sixth highest of all time and his total of 1,888 runs scored the 12th highest.

He was elected to the Baseball Hall of Fame in a special election in 1939. In 1969, the Baseball Writers of America voted him the Greatest First Baseman of All Time and his memory was honored with the issuance of a United States postage stamp in1989.

Lou Gehrig spent a lot of his career in the shadow of his team mate the great Babe Ruth but accomplished as much in his relatively short career as many of the greatest players of all time did in much longer careers.

SECTION 50

Yogi Berra of the New York Yankees holds the record for the most World Series games played in with 75. Not surprisingly, Yankees hold the next six places on this list with Mickey Mantle second at 65, Elston Howard, 54, Gil McDougald, 53, Hank Bauer, 53, Phil Rizzuto, 52 and Joe DiMaggio, 51.

BABE RUTH

Babe Ruth's plaque at the Baseball Hall of Fame says ' Greatest drawing card in history of baseball. Holder of many home run and other records. Gathered 714 home runs in addition to fifteen in World Series'. This may be the greatest under statement in the history of the game.

Born George Herman Ruth, in Baltimore, Maryland, on February 6, 1895, he was in a class by himself when it came to playing baseball. His team mate Joe Dugan was quoted on the Babe's page at the Hall of Fame as having once said ' To understand him you had to understand this: He wasn't human.'

Babe Ruth had two baseball careers. In his first, he was a starting pitcher with the Boston Red Sox from 1914 to 1919. In that period, he won 89 games and lost just 46 with a 2.19 ERA, starting 143 games and pitching 105 complete games.

In his second, which overlapped the first somewhat as he both pitched and played the outfield in it, and which lasted from 1914-1919, with the Red Sox, from 1920-1934 with the New York Yankees and 1935, with the Boston Braves, he had a career batting average of .342, got 2,873 hits, including 714 home runs and drove in 2,214 runs.

He is the only player in the history of baseball to have pitched a shut out in the World Series and to have had more than one home run in a single World Series game. Babe hit three home runs in one series game twice and hit two home runs in one game twice as well. Reggie Jackson, Albert Pujols and Pablo Sandoval are the only other players who have hit three in one series game.

He made his debut as a pitcher for the Red Sox on July 11, 1914, pitching seven innings against the Cleveland Naps, who became the Indians the following year, and giving up just two runs on eight hits for the win. He pitched in just four games that year, winning two and losing one as the Sox finished second 8 ½ games behind the Philadelphia Athletics.

In 1915, Babe won 18 and lost 8 as the Sox won the American League pennant and then beat the Athletics, four games to one, in the World Series. The Boston pitching staff was so strong, with Ernie Shore and Rube Foster both winning 19 and losing 8 and Dutch Leonard winning 15 and losing 7, that Babe never pitched in that series.

In 1916, he won 23 and lost 12 with a 1.75 ERA and the Sox won the pennant and bested the Brooklyn Robins in the World Series, four games to one. The Babe started and threw a complete game 14 innings in Game 2 as the Sox won 2-1. He gave up a home run to Brooklyn's center fielder Hi Myers with two out in the first and held them scoreless for the next 13 1/3 innings, for his first World Series win.

In 1917, he won 24 and lost 13, with a 2.01 ERA, as the Sox finished second behind the Chicago White Sox. The next year, 1918, the Sox won the pennant again and Babe won 13 and lost 7, with a 2.22 ERA. He also played 59 games in the outfield and 13 at first base that year, batting .300 and leading the league in homers with 11.

In the World Series against the Chicago Cubs, that year, he pitched a complete game, six hit shutout, to win Game 1, 1-0, and extend his scoreless innings streak in the World Series to 22 1/3 innings. In Game 4, he went 7 1/3 innings scoreless before the Cubs scored, giving him 29 2/3 consecutive scoreless innings, a World Series record at the time. That record was broken by the Yankees Whitey Ford in 1961. The Sox won that game 3-2, Babe got the win and the Sox went on to win the series four games to two.

In 1919, Babe won just 9 and lost 5, with a 2.97 ERA but played in 130 games, including 111 in the outfield and five at first base, batting .322 and winning the league home run title with 29 and leading the league with 113 RBI's. Everyone had finally realized that, as good a pitcher as he was, he was more valuable as an every day player.

Unfortunately for the Red Sox, their ownership had a money problem after the 1919 season and was forced to sell the Babe to the Yankees. Of course, this sale marked the beginning of the myth of the Curse of the Bambino as Red Sox fans over the years blamed the sale of the Babe for the drought in World Series wins the Sox experienced.

The Yankees immediately made Babe their right fielder and all he did was play 142 games, hit .376 and led the league in homers with 54, RBI's 135, runs scored 158, slugging percentage .847 and on base percentage .532. The Yankees finished in third that year, three games behind the pennant winning Cleveland Indians.

In 1921, he led the Yankees to the first of three successive pennants, hitting .378 with 59 homers and 168 RBI's. His 59 homers were more than 14 of the 15 Major League teams had for a total that year. In the World Series, which the Yankees lost to the New York Giants, five games to three, Ruth went just 5-16.

In 1922, the Yankees won the pennant again and were again defeated by the Giants four games to none with one tie. The Babe hit only .315 that year and his home run total fell to 35 with only 96 RBI's.

In 1923, he hit .393 and led the league in homers, 41, and RBI's, 130, and was the league's Most Valuable Player. The Yankees beat the Giants that year in the World Series, four games to two, and Babe went 7-19 at the plate with three homers.

He played with the Yankees for 15 years, from 1920-1934, during that time, he averaged .349 at the plate, hit 659 home runs, an average of 44 per year, had 1,978 RBI's, an average of 132 per year, and had a slugging percent age of .711 and an on base percentage of .484.

If he had played the outfield while with the Red Sox and hit homers at the rate he did as an outfielder with the Yankees, he would have hit 880 home runs in his career.

Babe's career numbers as a hitter are staggering. His career slugging percentage of .690 is 57 points higher than Ted Williams' who has the second highest career total of all time. He had a slugging percentage over .700 in nine different years. He had the highest career OPS, slugging plus on base percentage, total, ever at 1.164, beating Williams' 1.116. He led the American League in home runs 12 times, walks 11 times, runs scored eight times and RBI's five times. He hit over 40 home runs 11 times and over 50 four times.

In 1927, he set the record of 60 homers in a season that would last until Roger Maris hit 61 in 1961. In 1927, the average number of home runs hit by every other entire TEAM in the American League was 50. In six different season, he had over 135 RBI's and 135 bases on balls. In all of baseball history only six other players have ever had that many walks and RBI's in the same season and none of them have done it more than once.

He was in three World Series with the Red Sox as a pitcher and seven with the Yankees as a position player. His teams won seven of those World Series. After losing two of three to the Giants from 1921-1923, Babe and the Yankees were in the Series in 1926, losing to the Cardinals, 1927, beating the Pirates and 1928, beating the Cardinals. In 1932, they beat the Cubs for the Babe's seventh World Championship.

In the five Series' that he was in from 1923 through 1932, the Babe hit .400 with 34 hits in 85 at bats and 14 home runs and the Yankees won four of the five.

The numbers, as I said before, are staggering. Many people argue that today's players are bigger, faster and stronger than in previous eras and as many argue that the only true measure of players is by comparing their statistics against their contemporaries. No matter how you compare Babe Ruth's statistics or who you compare them against there is no question that George Herman Ruth, whether you call him Babe, the Sultan of Swat, the Colossus of Clout or any one of the other nick names people made up for this bigger than life hero, perhaps the best known athlete of all time, he was the best.

As the famous sports writer Tommy Holmes once wrote ' Some twenty years ago, I stopped talking about the Babe for the simple reason that I realized that those who had never seen him didn't believe me'.

Appropriately, Babe was in the first group of players elected to the Baseball Hall of Fame in 1936. Elected, along with him, were Ty Cobb, Walter Johnson, Christy Mathewson and Honus Wagner.

Made in the USA
San Bernardino, CA
28 March 2016